DESTINY BY DESIGN

THE CONSTRUCTION OF THE PANAMA CANAL

Destiny By Design

The Construction of the Panama Canal

Jeremy Sherman Snapp

FEATURING PHOTOGRAPHS BY
GERALD FITZGERALD SHERMAN
JEREMY SHERMAN SNAPP

PACIFIC HERITAGE PRESS
Lopez Island, WA USA

HERITAGE HOUSE
Surrey, B.C. Canada

Published in the United States of America by
Pacific Heritage Press
479 Old Homestead Road
Lopez Island, WA 98261

Library of Congress Cataloguing-in-Publication Data

Snapp, Jeremy Sherman, 1954-
    Destiny by design : the construction of the Panama Canal / Jeremy Sherman ; featuring photographs
    by Gerald Fitzgerald Sherman, Jeremy Sherman Snapp.

    Includes bibliographical references and index.
    ISBN 0-9673633-5-7 (alk. paper)
    1. Panama Canal (Panama) - Pictorial works. 2. Panama Canal (Panama) - History. 3. Canals -
    Panama - Panama Canal - Design and construction - History. 5. Americans - Panama - Panama
    Canal - History.
    I. Sherman, Gerald Fitzgerald, b. 1871. II Title.

F1569.C2.S63 2000   972.87'5'0222--dc21   00-062392
Publishing in Canada by
Heritage House Publishing Co. Ltd.
#108 - 17665 66A Avenue
Surrey, B.C. V3S 2A7

Canadian Cataloguing in Publication Data

Snapp, Jeremy Sherman, 1954-
    Destiny by design

    Includes bibliographical references and index.
    ISBN 894384-13-X (Heritage House)–ISBN 0-9673633-5-7 (Pacific Heritage Press)

    1. Panama Canal (Panama)–History–Pictorial works. 2. Canal zone–Pictorial works. I. Title.
F1569.C2S52 2000   972.87'5'00222   C00-0910845-9

Heritage House acknowledges the support of Heritage Canada, the Book Publishing Industry Development Program and the British Columbia Arts Council.

Cover and book design by Jeremy Sherman Snapp
Edited by Audrey McClellan
Layout by Darlene Nickull
Ship drawings on pages 158 and 159 by Keith Sternberg
Culebra cut photos, pages 113-119 by J.W.W., 1914

Printed in Singapore

"IT IS NOT THE CRITIC WHO COUNTS, NOT THE MAN WHO POINTS OUT HOW THE STRONG MAN STUMBLED, OR WHERE THE DOER OF DEEDS COULD HAVE DONE THEM BETTER. THE CREDIT BELONGS TO THE MAN WHO IS ACTUALLY IN THE ARENA; WHOSE FACE IS MARRED BY DUST AND SWEAT AND BLOOD; WHO STRIVES VALIANTLY, WHO ERRS AND COMES SHORT AGAIN AND AGAIN; WHO KNOWS THE GREAT ENTHUSIASMS, THE GREAT DEVOTIONS, AND SPENDS HIMSELF IN A WORTHY CAUSE; WHO, AT THE BEST, KNOWS IN THE END THE TRIUMPH OF HIGH ACHIEVEMENT; AND WHO, AT THE WORST, IF HE FAILS, AT LEAST FAILS WHILE DARING GREATLY, SO THAT HIS PLACE SHALL NEVER BE WITH THOSE COLD AND TIMID SOULS WHO KNOW NEITHER VICTORY NOR DEFEAT."   THEODORE ROOSEVELT

DEDICATION

This book is dedicated to the thousands of people who helped construct the Panama Canal and especially to the legions of laborers who lost their lives in the process.

ACKNOWLEDGEMENTS

The 120 photos made by my great-grandfather in April 1912 in Panama formed the basis of this book. We are fortunate that my cousin, John Sherman, preserved Gerald Sherman's photographs and papers and I am grateful for his permission to publish these photos.

I would also like to thank the many people who helped me put together the fascinating story to go with these historic photographs. The Sociedad Historica de Panama (Panama Historical Society) was very helpful, particularly Vincente Pascual, who is writing a book on the history of the U.S. military in the Canal Zone, 1903-1999; Nina Kosik, a lifelong Canal Zone resident and historian; Jason Critides and his father Leonidas Critides of Islamorada Int. S.A., who became my Canal Zone guides during my time in Panama; dredge captain Jay Gibson and his wife Llori; and Nico, a café owner and historian who helped with photo identification. The Technical Resources Center in Balboa, with its Panama Canal Collection, was also helpful.

I appreciate the help I received from the Panama Canal Museum in Seminole, Florida; from James L. Shaw, marine historian, whose book *The Ships of the Panama Canal* was most informative; from Captain Jeff Dyer, who gave me an understanding of what it takes to transit the canal in a Panamax ship; from Captain Harold Huycke, marine historian and author, and Nicholas Jones for his editorial help.

Last but not least, I appreciate my family, who supported me during another project, and particularly my son Trevor Townsend Snapp, who was so helpful during our time in Panama.

CONTENTS

FOREWORD

In 1966 I first caught sight of the Panama Canal not from the deck of a ship but from the window of a bus. I had been working in Costa Rica and was travelling to Panama to board a vessel at Colon, on Panama's Atlantic coast. In those days the Canal was surrounded by the Panama Canal Zone, an American enclave that seemed to "protect" the Canal against encroachment by Panama. The differences between the Zone and the host country were striking: well manicured lawns on one side and shanty town on the other. Today, control of the Canal is in Panamanian hands and although many of the differences still remain, changes are taking place. In *Destiny By Design* Jeremy Snapp provides us with a look at both the present and the past of this great engineering undertaking. His great-grandfather's photographs taken during the Canal's construction period offer insight into the immensity of the project and the conditions that had to be met. Gerald Fitzgerald Sherman made photograph in 1912 from an engineer's perspective: how the excavation was being accomplished, the equipment used and the methods employed. But he also took a number of "tourist" snapshots, capturing a shipboard deck scene while on his way to Panama, as well as views of buildings, docks and people once he arrived. Interestingly, Jeremy Snapp, his great-grandson, has blended in some of his own photograph taken at Panama in January 2000 and without referring to the Photograph Notes section (Page 164) it is often difficult to determine which is from the present and which is from the past. There have been changes along the Canal but at the same time, many things have stayed the same. Wander back then... and peer into history as one of the Great Wonders of the World is constructed.

James L. Shaw

Author, *Ships of the Panama Canal*

First-class battleship USS *Oregon*
(see following page)

INTRODUCTION

On the evening of 15 February 1898, the second-class battleship USS *Maine* exploded and sank, with the loss of 266 lives, at Havana, Cuba. At the time it was thought a Spanish harbor mine was responsible. This event helped precipitate the Spanish American War and launched the naval battle of Manila Bay on 1 May 1898.

In early March the first-class battleship USS *Oregon*, berthed at the naval shipyard at Bremerton, Washington, was ordered to San Francisco to take on coal and a load of ammunition. Fearing an imminent naval battle in the Caribbean, the U.S. War Department ordered the *Oregon* to Key West, Florida, a voyage of about 12,000 miles. Departing San Francisco on 19 March 1898, she headed south towards Cape Horn with a full head of steam. Transiting the Straits of Magellan and heading north against storm-force head winds, she averaged over 11 knots during her 58 days at sea and arrived at Key West 67 days later, on 27 May 1898, a record time. Taking on 1,760 tons of coal in her bunkers and another 200 tons in sacks on her main deck, she immediately steamed towards Havana, Cuba. She then proceeded towards Santiago de Cuba, where she engaged in the naval battle of Santiago and drove the Spanish battleship *Cristobal Colon* onto the Cuban coast at Turquino River on 3 July 1898.

Waiting four months, March to July, for the *Oregon*'s arrival at Cuba convinced America's leaders of the need for a canal through the Central American isthmus. Such a canal would have cut 8,000 miles from the *Oregon*'s voyage. President Theodore Roosevelt, a supporter of Manifest Destiny, was particularly influenced by Captain Alfred Thayer Mahan and his book *The Influence of Sea Power Upon History 1660-1783*, published in 1890. Captain (later Admiral) Mahan argued that the Caribbean Sea, as the American Mediterranean, needed to be connected to the Pacific by a canal as part of America's naval highway, mentioning the idea of an isthmian canal several times in his book.

The advantage of a route through the Isthmus of Panama had been recognized by Europeans soon after they arrived in the region. The native people had established a trail in the same area many years before the Spaniards arrived.

Rodrigo de Bastidas of Seville, Spain, was the first European to explore Panama in 1501. In 1502 he was followed by Christopher Columbus, who was told by the natives of a great sea, one week's journey away. It was nearly a decade later before Vasco Núñez de Balboa actually sighted the Pacific Ocean from Panama on 26 September 1513.

Spain is credited with establishing the first European-built "road" across the isthmus, the Las Cruces Trail, built in 1530. It linked Fort San Lorenzo with Panama City, partly via the Chagres River. Four years later, Charles V of Spain ordered a survey for a ship canal from the Chagres to the Pacific, following Alvaro Saavedra's drawings for a canal across the isthmus from 1529. This was not built, but in 1540 the Spaniards did build the Camino Real from Panama City to Porto Bello and Nombre de Dios.

On 16 October 1831, Captain George Peacock, master of HM Corvette *Hyacinth*, a survey ship on West Indian station, was sounding Chagres Roads. Concluding that the soundings on the existing Admiralty chart were incorrect, he continued further, entering Limon Bay the next day. With permission of Royal Navy commander William Oldrey, Peacock continued his survey inland through the lowlands as far as Gatun. After consulting with the natives, he realized the land continued fairly level all the way to Gorgona, more than halfway to Panama City. On 19 October he took a cayuco (dugout canoe) up the Chagres River, continued overland all the way to Panama, surveyed the Río Grande estuary there, and returned on 25 October. Peacock then departed, but returned on 23 February 1832 and, with another survey party, headed inland for

Busts of Ferdinand de Lesseps and Theodore Roosevelt on display at the Panama Canal Administration Building at Balboa Heights.

Panama. He gained more valuable information and returned a third time in February 1842 to complete his feasibility study of a canal and railroad. The Panama Railroad and the canal were eventually built very close to his proposed route (see the map on page 15).

General Ulysses S. Grant made seven expeditions to Panama between 1870 and 1875. Captain Edward P. Lull of the United States Navy surveyed the isthmus in 1875 and estimated a sea to sea lock canal being 42 miles in length.

The French attempt to construct a canal at Panama between 1881 and 1889 was headed by Vicomte Ferdinand de Lesseps, the man responsible for the French construction of the Suez Canal, which opened in 1869. A hero in France, de Lesseps convinced everyone there that a canal could be built in Panama with no more effort than it took to construct the Suez Canal. The valiant attempt at a sea-level canal in Panama, besides ending the lives of 22,000 workers, resulted in bankruptcy and scandal for the French Compagnie Universelle du Canal Interocéanique. In fairness to the French, it is doubtful that any nation would have succeeded in the 1880s, the conditions encountered at Panama being far more difficult than at Suez.

In 1889, the same year the French stopped work at Panama, the Maritime Canal Company was formed in the U.S. with the idea of constructing a Nicaraguan canal over the San Juan route, incorporating Lake Nicaragua. Purchasing equipment from the French at Panama, the Americans set to work constructing an 11-mile-long railroad, and with six dredges they removed 728,000 cubic yards of spoil before giving up in 1892.

By 1902 the French were desperately seeking to sell their entire operation in Panama. At this time the Americans were leaning towards building the canal in Nicaragua. However, the French lowered their asking price from $109 million to $40 million, which was precisely the value determined by the U.S. Walker Commission (set up to establish the best route for the canal). The price included the Panama Railroad, rights to build a canal, the work performed by the French, much equipment, and valuable survey information on river levels and the canal route. America decided to continue where the French had begun.

Gerald Sherman preparing for a mining survey, circa 1912.

On 28 June 1902, Congress passed the Spooner Act authorizing the president to proceed with the construction of the canal at Panama. After negotiating with Colombia and not reaching a canal agreement in 1903, the U.S. supported Panama's revolution and break with Colombia on 3 November 1903. Philippe Bunau-Varilla, a young engineer during the French period at Panama, desperately wanted to restore French honor and carry on "the great idea of Panama." He nearly single-handedly started the revolution, supplying the rebels in Panama with $100,000 and drumming up support in America.

By an interesting coincidence, the cruiser USS *Nashville* just happened to be at Colón during the uprising and was soon joined by the cruiser USS *Atlanta*, the new battleship USS *Maine*, the presidential yacht *Mayflower*, the USS *Prairie*, and the USS *Dixie*. Offshore of Panama City were the battleship USS *Wyoming*, the cruiser USS *Boston*, the USS *Concord*, and the USS *Marblehead*. Though Colombia did send three gunboats to Panama Bay—the *Bogota,* the *Padilla*, and the *Chucuito*—and the Colombian gunboat *Cartagena* did land troops at Colón, they all returned to Colombia lacking coal. There was only one casualty, a Chinese laundryman. The U.S. recognized the new republic three days later, on 6 November 1903.

President Roosevelt was anxious to "make the dirt fly," and a canal agreement (the Hay-Bunau-Varilla treaty) with the new republic of Panama was signed 12 days later, on 18 November. Roosevelt, who often quoted the West African expression "Speak softly and carry a big stick, you will go far," actually spoke *loudly* and carried a big stick. A strong proponent of U.S. imperialism, he believed the build-up of the U.S. Navy and the construction of an isthmian canal were imperative. In November 1906 he visited the Canal Zone, becoming the first president to leave the U.S. while in office. Roosevelt later commented, "I took the Isthmus, started the canal and then left congress not to debate the canal, but to debate me"

There were many designs for the 50-mile-long canal. In Paris in May 1879, at the Congrès International d'Etudes du canal Interocéanique, Baron Adolphe Godin de Lépinay was the first to suggest a lock canal with navigable lakes at each end, but he was not taken seriously. Ferdinand de Lesseps was determined to build a sea-level canal, following Lieutenant Wyse's survey, near the railroad line. Just before bankruptcy, de Lesseps enlisted Alexandre Gustave Eiffel to design a lock canal, with lock dimensions of 59 by 590 feet. When the Americans started work in Panama, a final design had not been agreed upon, and it was not until John Stevens became chief engineer in 1905 that the present lock canal design, with Lake Gatun at an 85-foot altitude, was adopted.

By 11 November 1904, when the first American steam shovel began work at Culebra Cut, Americans were fascinated by the project. Thousands later visited the canal, and by 1912, 20,000 people were visiting the isthmus annually. My great-grandfather, American mining engineer Gerald Sherman, was one of those visitors. An avid photographer with some engineering contacts, he was able to photograph from many vantage points not open to tourists. This resulted in a magnificent collection of construction photographs of the entire length of the canal, made during the month of April 1912.

The Panama Canal has always fascinated me, and in January 2000, right after the U.S. formally turned over the canal to Panama, I had the opportunity to spend some time there with my son Trevor. It was the perfect time to photograph the end of the American era and the beginning of the Panamanian era.

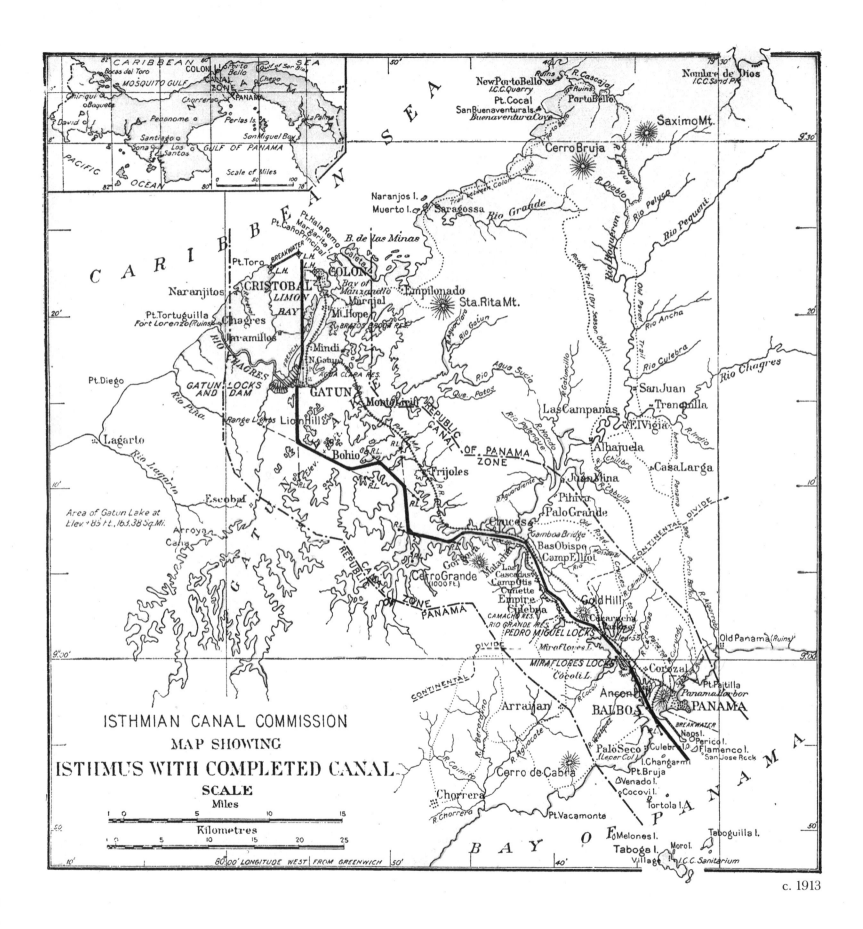

ISTHMIAN CANAL COMMISSION
MAP SHOWING
ISTHMUS WITH COMPLETED CANAL
SCALE
Miles
Kilometres

c. 1913

13

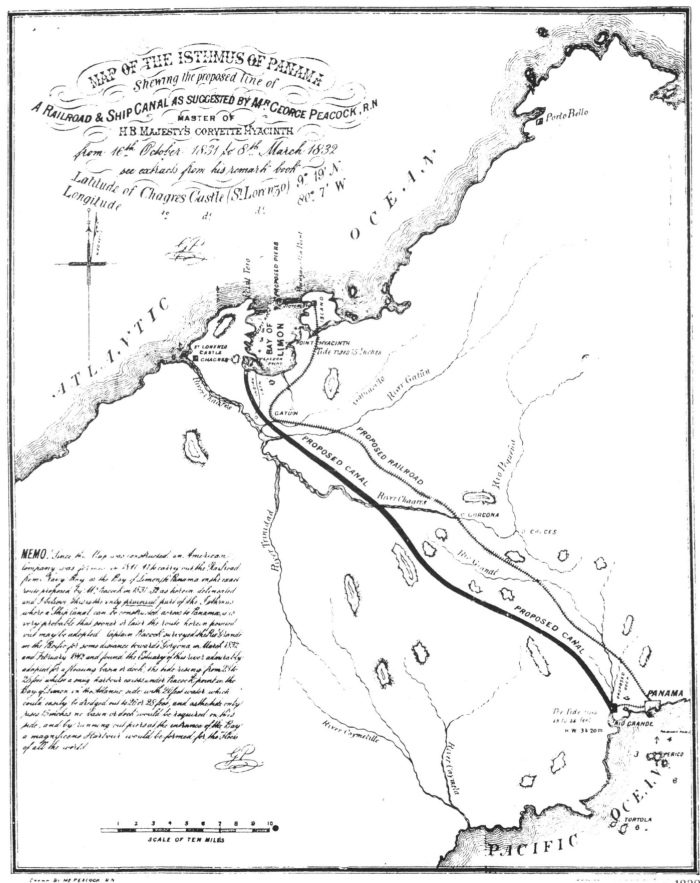

c. 1832

15

THE SPANISH MAIN

When Cristóbal Colón (Christopher Columbus) sailed west across the Atlantic Ocean in 1492, he was searching for a route to the far east, the Cipango (Japan), Cathay (China), and India. He offered the Spanish Crown a vision and theory that it was possible to arrive in the east by sailing west–a theory that seemed reasonable to learned men.

By 1420 the Portuguese had begun a settlement in Madeira, but they had no plans to sail farther west. Queen Isabella of Spain supported Admiral Columbus, and he left Palos, Spain, on 3 August 1492 on the *Santa María*, voyaging with two slightly smaller caravels, the *Pinta* and *Niña*. Arriving at the Canary Islands eight days later, they prepared their ships for the long voyage ahead, departing about 5 September.

After a 33-day ocean crossing, land was sighted on 12 October 1492. This was one of the Bahama Islands, which was named San Salvador. Columbus, convinced that he had discovered India and China, then sailed through the Caribbean for several months, on the lookout for gold, spices and slaves. (He had agreed to give the Spanish Crown one fifth of his profits.) He discovered Juana (Cuba) and Hispaniola (Haiti), where the *Santa María* hit a reef and sank on the northern coast. The settlement of Navidad was started there with 39 men from the *Santa María*. Columbus returned to Palos on 15 March 1493.

On 15 September 1493, Columbus left on his second voyage to the New World with a fleet of 17 ships and 1,500 men, making the crossing in 20 days. He discovered Puerto Rico and the Leeward Islands on his return to Navidad. None of the men left at the settlement had survived, so Columbus started another outpost, a little to the east, called Isabella.

Returning to Spain in March 1496, Columbus showed the king and queen samples of gold and assured them the colonies would be profitable soon. Departing again in May 1498 with six caravels, he arrived at Isabella and Santo Domingo to find gold production slim and the Indians keeping the Spaniards alive. By 1499, though taking pride in his discoveries, the Crown was convinced Columbus was a romantic living in a world of wishful thinking, and on 14 May 1499 Francisco de Bobadilla was named governor of the Indies.

Though stripped of authority, Columbus was still Admiral of the Ocean Sea, and he sailed from Cádiz, Spain, with four ships on 11 May 1502, arriving at the island of Martinique on 15 June. Escaping a hurricane at Ocoa Bay, he sailed past Cuba towards Honduras and south along the Mosquito Coast, stopping at Caraiay (Puerto Limon) on 25 September. Continuing along the coast of Veragua (later known as New Granada, Colombia, and finally Panama), Columbus arrived at Porto Bello on 2 November 1502. On 10 November he entered Bastimientos, or Retrete. This bay had been discovered about two years earlier by the first European to explore Panama, Rodrigo de Bastidas, with Vasco Núñez de Balboa as first mate. In 1510 Diego de Nicuesa renamed Retrete, calling it Nombre de Dios, Name Of God.

Columbus attempted to establish a colony at Río Belen in 1503. Although he was unsuccessful and lost two ships on the Panama coast, he had set a course for every other exploration of the Spanish Main. He died in May 1506, not realizing he had discovered a new continent.

Many historic sites of the Spanish Main, such as Fort San Lorenzo, are still visible. Built in the later years of the 16th century, it was destroyed and rebuilt many times.

This view from the fort looking southeast shows the mouth of the Chagres River. The Chagres was the main highway into central Panama, and it was common to navigate the river as far as Las Cruces and then travel by mule on the Las Cruces Trail across the continental divide to Old Panama. The square concrete plate at left most likely covers an old Spanish well.

Henry Morgan's pirates defeated the Spaniards at Fort San Lorenzo prior to sacking Old Panama in January 1671. Upon his return, Morgan razed the remains of the fort. Rebuilt in 1751, it never regained its former importance. When Colón became the Atlantic terminus of the Panama Railroad about 1855, the Royal Mail Steam Packet Company ships stopped calling at Chagres, a nearby village of about fifty bohío (thatched roof houses), built around an iron-roofed church, and it disappeared.

The sentry box, with magazine below, at Fort San Lorenzo was rebuilt along with the rest of the fort in the 1750s and looks well preserved today. Though the fort was rebuilt to the same plan as the original one, no wood was used in the reconstruction.

This southeast view shows the Spanish cannon of Fort San Lorenzo and the mouth of the Chagres River. The iron cannon are original to the late 18th century.

The remains of Fort Porto Bello are seen here, with Spanish cannon. After Francis Drake destroyed fortifications at Nombre de Dios, the Caribbean end of the Camino Real, in 1572, the terminus was moved to Porto Bello, a few miles to the west, and a fort was built there.

Porto Bello was taken over by the English admiral Edward Vernon about 1738, along with Fort San Lorenzo. The Spanish rebuilt both forts about 13 years later. The church to the right of the sally port is not an original Spanish-built church. It is used today for Porto Bello's "Black Christ" festivals.

A piragua (dugout canoe) arrives at Porto Bello. Discovered by Columbus on 2 November 1502 during his last voyage to the Spanish Main, Porto Bello was so named because of its large harbor and beautiful, cultivated shores, dotted with many bohío. It was an important Spanish stronghold and served as the main port for transshipment of gold and silver from Peru, through Panama via the Camino Real, to Spain.

Starting about 1910, the Isthmian Canal Commission quarried large rocks across the bay from Fort Porto Bello, to be used in construction of a breakwater at Limon Bay. A rock-crushing operation was also set up there, and rock was barged to Gatun for making concrete used in lock construction.

The first Panama City, Panamá la Vieja (Old Panama) was founded by the greedy Pedro Arias Dávila (Pedrarias) in August of 1519 after he had executed Vasco Núñez de Balboa. Pedrarias later stole the ships that Balboa had built on the Pacific coast.

Balboa was the first European to sight the great South Sea, the Pacific Ocean, on 27 September 1513, near Golfo de San Miguel. He was on his way to more discoveries when killed by the jealous Pedrarias.

Though today Panama City has grown all the way to Old Panama, many ruins of the old city survive. One of the surviving ruins is Cabildo de la Ciudad, the City Hall, shown here.

One of the better-preserved examples of Old Panama is the tower of the Catedral de Nuestra Señora de la Asunción (Our Lady of the Ascension Cathedral). Originally constructed of wood in 1585, it was rebuilt with stone in 1626, but destroyed by fire on 21 February 1644. Rebuilt again in 1649, it burned a final time when Henry Morgan sacked Panama on 28 January 1671, and was abandoned.

Pedrarias's choice of location for Panama City lacked a protected harbor and fields to cultivate crops. It was always dependent on imported food. With Balboa's ships, Pedrarias sent some men to Natá to secure food from the native people, who were growing maize and other food crops. The Iglesia y Convento de Santo Domingo (Church and Convent of St. Dominic) is shown above.

Casas Reales, or the Royal Houses, with their heavily constructed walls, were built for defense, but the Spaniards couldn't stand up to Morgan and his men. Though Old Panama contained thousands of buildings and a population of about 30,000, it was abandoned after Morgan's sacking. A new city was built in 1673 on a point about five miles to the southwest, considered easier to defend. As Panama City grew to the northeast, the old Spanish colonial townsite became known as Casco Viejo (Old Compound).

Puente del Rey, the Bridge of the King, spans the Río Abajo at the northern part of Old Panama. About 450 years old, it survives today. Continuing north along the Camino Real, constructed in 1540, a traveler would arrive at Nombre de Dios, and in later years at Porto Bello.

A piragua or cayuco is poled up the Chagres River. These forms of native dugout canoe are still made today from espave, caoba, or cedro amargo (mahogany and cedar). For centuries they were the most common way to transport people or goods. Note the bohío, or native-style thatched house, in the center of the photo. These were always built well above ground. Though this photo was made in 1912, the style of travel and style of house were basically the same as at the time of the Spanish Main.

VOYAGE TO PANAMA

Visitors to Panama in the early years of the 20th century had one travel option: a voyage by ship. Upon arrival on the Atlantic side of Panama, American ships generally docked at Cristóbal, inside the U.S. Canal Zone. New concrete piers were built there in 1906 to handle the extra shipping due to canal construction. Founded by the French about 1880, Cristóbal was separated only by a narrow firebreak from the wood-frame buildings of Colón. Cristóbal was the site of the Panama Canal railroad shops, a cold storage plant, a coaling station, a French-built hospital, and a hotel. From Cristóbal or Colón, people would board the Panama Railroad for points south.

The nearest American port of embarkation was Key West, and the next nearest, New Orleans. The most traveled route, however, was from New York City. A constant flow of people and goods from New York to Colón and Cristóbal ensued when canal construction began. They traveled on several steamship lines, including the U.S.-government-owned Panama Railroad Company and its steamships *Ancon*, *Cristobal*, and *Panama*; the United Fruit Company with its British-flagged fleet; the Hamburg-American line; and the Royal Mail Steam Packet Company, chartered in 1839 with the purpose of linking England and the Caribbean. The Pacific Mail Steamship line had served both coasts since before the Panama Railroad was built. The Hamburg-American line made scheduled trips from New Orleans, and a traveler could also depart from Key West via the Peninsular and Occidental line. Other lines stopping at Colón included White Star, Red Cross, and North German Lloyd ships.

On the Pacific side, steamers departed from U.S. West Coast ports, and there was scheduled service from other countries, notably Peru and Chile in South America. Ships docked at La Boca, later called Balboa.

This sidewheel steamer with its exposed walking-beam engine is a relic of an earlier era. Built after the Civil War, this oceangoing steamer might originally have used an auxiliary sailing rig. Range under power with an inefficient steam engine was limited by the size of the coal bunker. Vessels of this type steamed to Panama in the nineteenth century. They had mostly retired by the time of the American construction era.

New Orleans was a popular port of embarkation on the Gulf of Mexico for passage to Colón. Steamers such as the one above were typical of the vessels carrying passengers and freight to Panama for the canal project. This steamship was the latest thing compared to the steamer on the previous page.

Most passengers on this route were tourists, American skilled labor, or engineers. They enjoyed several days of Caribbean voyaging before arriving at Colón, engaging in games like shuffleboard aboard the United Fruit Company steamer *Parismina*, above.

The United Fruit Company began in 1899 when plantation owner Minor Keith joined in partnership with the Boston Fruit Company to form the largest agricultural company in the world. Keith owned thousands of acres of banana plantations at Bocas del Toro on Chiriquí Lagoon, west of Colón. The population of Bocas del Toro grew from a few people to about 9,000 by 1912.

United's Great White Fleet transported all the bananas to market. United added two passenger steamers to its fleet in response to extra passenger demand during the canal construction. Though the company was American, all its ships were British flagged.

This view of Colón from about a mile northwest of Manzanillo Point could be seen just prior to docking at the Cristóbal wharves (next page). Colón boomed when it became the Caribbean terminus of the Panama Railroad, but it never lost its reputation as a shantytown. Note the navigational light tower, marking Manzanillo Point, at the center of the photo. At the extreme left is the Episcopalian Christ-Church-by-the-Sea, the oldest church in Colón, and nearby is the New Washington Hotel.

John L. Stephens, one of the founders of the Panama Railroad, named the town Aspinwall (after one of his partners) at the time the Americans were constructing the railroad. The French called it Colón, however, and Colombians insisted on using the French name and would not deliver mail addressed to Aspinwall.

The Panama Railroad steamship *Ancon* is offloading cargo at Cristóbal's Pier No. 11, immediately southwest of Colón. This twin-screw steamer of 9,600 tons was the first ship to officially transit the canal on 15 August 1914. Built in 1902 she was originally owned by the Boston Steamship Company.

Cristóbal was originally called Christophe-Colomb (Christopher Columbus) during the French period of construction. The large house at left was De Lesseps' residence during the French era. It later became a canal administration building and then the Cristobal Women's Club. In front of this building stood a bronze statue of Christopher Columbus and an Indian maiden. This gift from Empress Eugénie of France to the Republic of Colombia arrived in 1879. It is now located at the end of Colón's Central Avenue.

Arrivals and departures of passenger steamers were usually a big event at Cristóbal, as shown in this departure scene at Pier 11. It would be a long time before family and friends saw each other again.

This South American passenger steamer is likely taking on coal, possibly at the La Boca coaling station. The Panama Canal Company had a coal monopoly in Panama, with a 500,000-ton capacity at Cristóbal and a 200,000-ton capacity at La Boca. The coal was shipped down from Norfolk, Virginia, by private steamship lines.

This steamer possibly at the old wharf at La Boca is likely also there to take on coal. On 31 March 1923 the coal plant shut down, since by this time about 70 percent of the ships were using fuel oil. Note the windsails–large ventilators suspended from the rigging–commonly used to cool the below deck spaces aboard ships in the tropics. The La Boca wharf collapsed 17 August 1912, sinking the steamer *Newport* in the process.

At Home In Panama

Panama became independent from Spain in 1821. Though it later joined with New Granada (after 1861, Colombia), many Panamanians wanted to remain independent. Many revolutions were planned, and during the 50 years prior to its independence, a revolution was staged nearly every year.

One reason the Republic of Panama's 1903 revolution was successful was America's desire for an isthmian canal that would benefit the U.S. and other industrialized nations. Panama gained $10 million plus an annuity of $250,000 for the use of its land. The average Panamanian, however, received little if any benefit, and only a few helped in the construction of the canal. Some city dwellers profited from American investment, but the natives and other rural residents gained nothing.

Housing for canal workers was based on salary and was provided rent-free. The gold employees (Whites) lived in the best houses, while the silver employees (Blacks) were offered smaller cabins or barracks. Many Black families simply built their own shacks in the jungle.

Wages were high for the era. An unskilled laborer might make 9 cents an hour, while a skilled machinist would receive 38 cents an hour. At the other end of the scale, chief engineer John Stevens received $30,000 a year.

Before the Americans arrived in 1904, Panama was considered a death trap due to the prevalence of malaria, yellow fever, and other diseases. During the French construction era, most employees arriving on the isthmus never returned, but died and were buried in Panama. With the arrival of Dr. William C. Gorgas, chief sanitarian, that began to change. While stationed in Cuba, Gorgas demonstrated what Cuban physician Carlos Finlay had discovered in 1881: eradicating the *Aedes* mosquito could eliminate yellow fever. He eliminated the disease in eight months in Havana in 1901 and attacked it in Panama in 1904.

While he was working in India in 1901, English physician Ronald Ross found that the *Anopheles* mosquito spread malaria. Ross visited the isthmus in 1904 to advise Gorgas, who used this knowledge against malaria there. Gorgas had to fight for money to fund his mosquito brigades, as most people simply didn't believe mosquitos were the cause of diseases. He didn't give up, and in one year he brought both diseases under control by draining and treating standing water and through the use of copper screens. The last case of yellow fever was reported on 11 November 1905. Malaria was never completely eradicated.

Canal workers were from many different countries, though most came from Barbados, Jamaica, the U.S., Spain, Italy, and India. By March 1913 the workforce numbered about 53,600, including 8,900 sick or on leave and 5,000 working for the McClintic-Marshall Company building lock gates. There was high turnover, so medals were given to the 7,400 U.S. workers who had remained on the job for two years. These medals were struck from scrap bronze left by the French.

Except for the Panama Railroad, horse-drawn carriages were the usual form of transport during the canal construction era. Only a few automobiles were on the isthmus during this time.

Colón and Cristóbal were built on Manzanillo Island, which is just a couple of feet above sea level. Before the growth of Colón and Cristóbal, with their wharves and industrial areas, much of the island looked like this palm grove near the Isthmian Canal Commission Hospital.

Most tourists and people with business in Colón stayed at the New Washington Hotel. It was named New Washington so as not to confuse it with the old Washington House, and it opened for business at the northern tip of Manzanillo Island on 29 March 1912.

When in Panama City, most important people stayed at the Hotel Tivoli, built in 1906 on the southern slope of Ancon Hill. President Roosevelt was its first guest that year during his visit to Panama.

Wood-frame residences in Colón, built during the American era, still survive today. These wooden structures were generally built from Douglas fir, cedar, and redwood imported from the West Coast of the U.S. In 1885, during one of many revolutions here, Colón was completely destroyed by fire. Though rebuilt better than before, it was always a poor relation compared to Panama City.

These wooden structures are typical of the employee housing built by the Americans after Nombre de Dios was destroyed by fire in 1912, when sparks from a boiler caused a house to catch on fire.

Diego de Nicuesa tried to establish a fort at Nombre de Dios in 1510, but it wasn't until 1519, when Pedrarias reestablished the settlement, that it survived for any length of time. It was the Atlantic terminus of the Camino Real mule trail for over 50 years.

Two rivers flow into the Caribbean at Nombre de Dios: the Terrin and the Pato. Río Nombre de Dios is just a mile to the west. These rivers bring a tremendous amount of sand to the area, which was used in all concrete for construction on the Atlantic side. No ruins of the original Spanish settlement exist because of fires, floods, and the shifting sands of the delta area.

The black sand was mined from Nombre de Dios for many years and is still moved from here today, using an old American barge as a loading dock. Though this location is about 40 miles northeast of Gatun, suitable sand of quantity was not found any closer. During their search for sand, the canal engineers approached the San Blas natives, to the east of Nombre de Dios, to ask if they would sell the sand. The San Blas' response was that they could not give away or sell what God had given them, and the engineers were told to leave, end of discussion.

Gold employee housing such as this was built at Gorgona, Empire, and Culebra, though nothing much of these settlements exists today. During the height of canal construction, more people lived in this area (see the map on page 13) than in Panama City or Colón.

Culebra was the "capital" during the construction era. The administration building is at center left. The house at right, with its screened porches, was typical of gold employee housing at Culebra.

Gold employee housing is in the foreground, with silver housing in the background, likely at Empire. Smoke in the background is from steam-powered machinery working in the Culebra Cut.

Panama City as viewed from Ancon Hill. The Pacific entrance to the canal is at right. The size of the city remained stable until explosive growth after World War II and it eventually encompassed Old Panama.

The original site of Panama City, now called Casco Viejo, was founded in 1673, two years after Henry Morgan sacked Old Panama. Viewed from the sea wall of the old fort, the two towers of the Panama Cathedral are visible at left. Its cornerstone was laid when the city was founded. Also located in the Parque Catedral (Cathedral Plaza) is the Municipal Building, whose round roof can be seen at left.

Though Casco Viejo shows its age, much of it is being restored today, including this hotel. Other major projects have included the old headquarters of the French Compagnie Universelle du Canal Interocéanique (now a museum), the National Theatre, Plaza Bolívar, and Plaza Herrera.

The Cathedral Plaza has been part of more than three centuries of history. Panamanian independence was declared here on 3 November 1903, and the plaza name was later changed to Plaza de la Independencia. Just visible at center is the cathedral and its towers. (Page 54)

This typically narrow street in Casco Viejo is near the Plaza de la Independencia. (Page 55)

THE ATLANTIC DIVISION

About one year after Colonel George W. Goethals of the U.S. Army was appointed chief engineer in 1907, he divided the canal project into three separate divisions: Atlantic, Central, and Pacific. The Atlantic division included construction of two great breakwaters at Limon Bay, the dredging of a 500-foot-wide approach channel, more than seven miles long, to the three locks at Gatun, and the building of Gatun Dam (see the map on page 13). The three double lock chambers were designed to raise a ship 85 feet, to the level of Lake Gatun, which was formed by Gatun Dam. All this was overseen by Major William Sibert.

The 11,600-foot west breakwater from Toro Point was constructed between 1910 and 1912, with 12- to 18-ton boulders quarried at Porto Bello. These were brought the 20 miles down the coast by tug and barge. Later a railroad trestle was constructed on the Limon Bay side, and shunted flatcars full of rock were unloaded there by the Lidgerwood plow. The 10,400-foot east breakwater from Margarita Island was constructed in similar fashion. However, the rock for the east breakwater was quarried at Sosa Hill and brought the 40 miles by flatcars. Later, 25-ton concrete blocks were also used to combat the fury of the recurring northerlies. The project was finally completed in 1916.

The approach channel was partly dredged by the French, who had maintained a navigation channel as far as the Cristóbal wharves. The suction dredge *Ancon*, sister-ship to the *Culebra*, removed an additional 13 million cubic yards between 1907 and 1912, working six days a week. Other vessels in the Atlantic dredging fleet included six pipeline suction dredges, two French and four American (one being the *Sandpiper*, see page 61); three rebuilt French ladder dredges (such as the *Gopher* and the *Mole*); two dipper dredges (such as the *Chagres*); one French clam-shell dredge; five rebuilt French self-propelled barges; two rebuilt French supply tenders; nine dump scows; one crane boat; one drill boat; four tugs; plus various lighters, launches, and pile drivers.

The dredging work was fairly routine, with two exceptions: the more difficult rock and hard clay encountered in the Mindi Hills, and the problems caused by flooding. With the tremendous rainfall on the Atlantic side and the ensuing floods, the tugs couldn't propel themselves, with barges in tow, up the canal. For weeks at a time they had to winch themselves towards the lock site, a few feet at a time.

By the summer of 1912 the Atlantic approach channel was complete, dredged to a depth of 41 feet. A total of 30,103,104 cubic yards had been dredged, along with 6,113,621 cubic yards excavated by steam shovel.

Gatun Dam was designed to be 105 feet above sea level, 1,700 feet wide, by 1.5 miles long. The idea was quite controversial at the time, since an earthen dam this size had never been built before. The dam created 163.4-square-mile Lake Gatun, making 22 miles of the Chagres River valley navigable, with relatively little dredging necessary in the ship channel.

Two sets of railroad track were laid, about a quarter mile apart, for trains that came to dump rock they brought from the Culebra Cut at Bas Obispo and from the cut through the Mindi Hills. This formed two toes, or walls, of the Gatun Dam. Suction dredges pumped silt between these toes to fill the interior of the dam.

The natural settling of the rock forming the two toes was sometimes dramatic, and the track was frequently relaid. This made great press, as critics of an earthen dam of this size used it as evidence that the dam would not stand up to the water pressure of Lake Gatun.

A suction dredge pumps spoil onto Gatun Dam. Note the steel pipe used for pumping the spoil.

The cutterhead suction dredge *Sandpiper* is pumping spoil into the center of Gatun Dam. The revolving cutterhead is lowered by the dredge's stiff-leg crane, at right. Large pumps move the liquid spoil produced by the cutterhead through the steel pipe floating above water level, at left.

The hydraulic pumping of fill from the Limon Bay channel began on 24 December 1908. The spoil flowed into the dam, filling the area between the toes, for several years.

On 25 April 1910, the west diversion of the Chagres River was closed off and the Chagres began to rise, creating Lake Gatun. Many islands of floating vegetation began to form. It was an interesting sight to watch tugs push these islands up onto the shore. Note the rail cars preparing to dump rock on top of the south toe.

This view northeast from Gatun Dam shows the waste weir. It was located about half a mile southwest of the southernmost lock. Note the Canal administration building at center right. The power station was built above the ten arches forming the power station spillway, at left.

The spillway is under construction, and Lake Gatun is forming at right. The lake had been slowly rising for about two years when this photo was made in 1912.

The spillway and weir are actually part of the Chagres River. The electric generating house at left supplied power for lock operations and is still in use today (see pages 142-143).

This view of Gatun Locks shows steel concrete forms at center and cableway towers in the background. The building at right was likely part of the concrete mixing operation.

Steel stored at Gatun (above) included 18-foot-diameter water tunnel forms, rectangular operating tunnel forms, and stacks of jacking plates. The forms were designed to be collapsible so they could be easily removed after the concrete had cured.

The three lock sites in the Panama Canal used different methods of moving the concrete to the construction areas. At Gatun, cableways (right) were employed. The cableway towers were 85 feet tall, traveled on railways, and were used in pairs. Six-ton buckets of concrete were brought to the towers by automated railway and were moved by way of the cables to where they were needed (see page 83).

The approach walls at Gatun Locks are nearly completed, and Lake Gatun is rising in the background.

Another view of the approach walls at Gatun Locks. Note the mast and lifting boom, with steam-powered winches and boiler in the little shed on top of the walls.

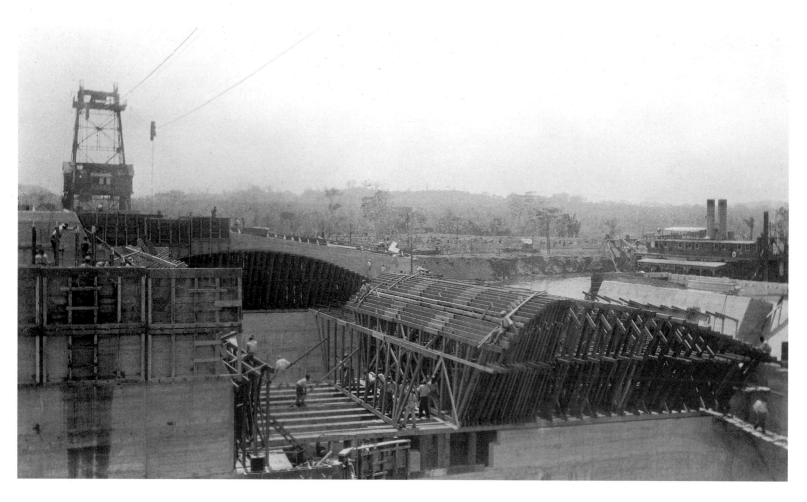

The construction of the locks took four years. The first concrete was poured at Gatun on 24 August 1909. Before concrete was poured from the buckets, forms were put in place. Here specially made spillway arch forms are being set up. A spillway arch has just been built in the background. At far right there is a dredge working the Gatun channel on the Limon Bay side of the locks.

A great variety of work is being performed at the Gatun Locks. Note the steam crane at center, used for lifting forms into place.

A total of 52 million gallons of water from the Chagres River pass through the 18-foot-diameter water tunnels (above) in the six locks of the canal (three near the Atlantic and three near the Pacific) every time a ship travels from ocean to ocean. The water moves entirely by gravity.

The operating tunnel (left) is in the center section between the two locks. It provides access to the electric motors and machinery that open and close the lock gates.

The photos on the next two pages show the gate chamber in the water tunnel. All this hardware, including over 18,000 roller bearings, was manufactured by the Wheeler Mold and Foundry Company. The valves in these huge culverts are comprised of two large steel gates sliding on roller bearings in a steel framework. These gates weigh ten tons each. When filling the double locks, the lower chamber valves are closed and the upper chamber valves open and gravity does the rest. To drain water from the lock, the opposite is done. A total of 114 rising stem valves and 120 cylindrical valves are used in operating all six locks.

Gatun Locks with the cableway towers in the background. In the foreground are iron plates used for plating the lock gates (see pages 88 through 95).

Looking south to the center wall tunnel. The locomotive tracks would be located at left and right on this wall. Note the space at the lower left of the photograph—this is for elevator access to the operating tunnel.

The three rising levels of the Gatun Lock floors are clearly visible here. There is a gate recess at left. Note the concrete buckets in the background being transported by the cableways.

This lock view shows the many chamber holes at the lock floor, which receives water from the cylindrical valve. This valve can permit inflow of water for half or full chamber spill. The locks are regularly drained for maintenance, and up to two tons of fish have been removed from the chamber holes.

The rails for the towing locomotives are at right. In the center of the tracks is the rack rail, or traction rail, which is gripped by the traction gear in the towing locomotive. The locomotives, or mules, tow the ships through the locks (see page 141).

This view of the Gatun Locks operating tunnel, looking north, shows the space before it was compartmentalized for the operating equipment. These two photos show the separate lock chambers, which can accommodate northbound and southbound traffic at the same time.

Another view of the center wall looking north, but from the next lock south. Compartments are being built to house the gate- and valve-operating machinery. Note the two pairs of cableways at left. Each pair moved in unison along the railway track to where concrete was needed.

The main concrete forms for the lock chambers were 36 feet wide and traveled on railroad tracks (above). Concrete is being dumped from a bucket at the top center of the photo. Recess for the gate leaf is at right.

Detail of a lock concrete form, at left.

The two temporary dams (above and left) at Gatun Locks on the Limon Bay side kept the sea at bay until everything was ready. The photo at left shows the forms still in place at the spillway arch, where concrete was recently poured.

The lock gates at Gatun, with a second pair directly behind the first for extra safety. The stiff-leg crane on top of the lock wall, beside the boxcar, was used for lowering material and equipment to the lock chamber floor.

A view of the same set of gates from the other side, on the lock floor. Note the temporary bridge above the lock gates. The design of the lock system is generally attributed to three men: Lt. Col. Harry Hodges, Henry Goldmark, and Edward Schildhauer. Goldmark was responsible for designing the lock miter gates.

The McClintic-Marshall Company of Pittsburgh, specializing in steel bridge construction, built the original 92 individual leaves of the lock miter gates in place (above and left). Others were built later as spares. The leaves were each 65 feet wide, 7 feet thick, and between 47 and 82 feet high. The tallest leaves, each weighing 745 tons, were used on the Pacific side of the Miraflores Locks because of the Pacific tides. Each leaf was built as a watertight vessel, which helped achieve a more neutral buoyancy in water, thereby requiring less power to open and close. Steel plating was riveted over the steel framework, similar to the "in and out" plating on a ship.

The immensity of the gates is apparent when one is standing on the floor of the lock chamber, and not so noticeable when the locks are full of water (above and left). Construction of the gates of Gatun commenced in May 1911 and ended two years later.

Shown above are three sets of gates in the upper Gatun Locks. By standing on the guard gate, the operating gates, the intermediary gates, and the safety gates can be seen. Two sets of gates are already plated, using thousands of rivets.

The lock gates, in the photo at left, are being plated. One of the more uncomfortable jobs was working inside the leaves, which had very little ventilation and heated up like an oven in the hot Panamanian sun. Nearly six million rivets were used in the 92 leaves. For many years repairs were made with the gates in place. Today they are sometimes towed to nearby shipyards like any other 745-ton steel vessel, and repairs are made there.

This view of the Gatun Locks, looking north, shows four pairs of cableways. Each pair used 2.5-inch steel cable, spanning 800 feet, to move the six-ton concrete buckets wherever they were needed.

On 28 July 1909 the cableways started operating, and on 24 August 1909 the first bucket of concrete was poured. A total of two million cubic yards of concrete were poured at the Gatun locks and they were finished on 21 May 1913. Note the steam-powered railway crane at left.

THE CENTRAL DIVISION

In 1905, John Frank Stevens replaced John Findley Wallace, who had been chief engineer of the Central division for about a year and wasn't making much headway. Stevens, who had been chief engineer for James Hill's Great Northern Railroad, arrived in Panama on 25 July 1905. He realized right away that removing millions of cubic yards of dirt and rock was not so much an excavation challenge as a transportation challenge. Within 18 months he had increased the railroad from 73 miles to 350 miles. He also increased the amount of general rolling stock from 35 to 293, and of flatcars from 560 to 3,915.

Major David DuBose Gaillard was in charge of this largest division of the canal, which covered the 32 miles between Gatun and Pedro Miguel Locks. The 8.75-mile-long Culebra Cut received most of the world's attention, but the Chagres River valley also had to be prepared for Lake Gatun. Whole villages—notably Bohío, Frijoles, Lagarto, and Ahorca—were moved, and about 7 million cubic yards were excavated along the canal route. The rising waters were watched with some apprehension, for it was most important the new lake be watertight. In some areas of the perimeter, such as the Trinidad Valley, the height of the rim was increased with fill.

The Culebra Cut took the most effort, as the 312-foot-high pass through the Cordillera Central had to be excavated to a depth of about 45 feet above sea level. A total of 147 million cubic yards were excavated by the French and the Americans between 1881 and 1913, with the Americans removing about two thirds of that figure. This was more than anyone anticipated because of the nearly continuous (26) slides, which necessitated a much lower angle of repose in many areas. In all, over 25 million cubic yards were excavated from the cut due to slides. The Cucaracha slide was active for about 30 years.

In January 1913, two slides totaling a million cubic yards fell into the cut, and Gaillard broke under the strain. By the end of the year Gaillard, found to be suffering from a brain tumor, was dead and never saw the completion of his work. The death of this well-liked, devoted man was mourned for a long time, and years later the name Culebra Cut was changed to Gaillard Cut in his honor.

Tom Starr contemplates the immensity of the Culebra Cut. Gold Hill rises up behind him, exceeding the angle of repose for this area of the Culebra Cut. On 20 January 1913 about a million tons of rock cascaded off this hill just three days after 400,000 yards slid down the Cucaracha slide on the opposite side.

The French referred to this spot as Culebra, the snake, but to the Americans, Culebra referred to the entire nine-mile cut.

Gold Hill is on the right, with Contractors Hill at left, looking northwest. It was thought gold might be located at Gold Hill, but it didn't pan out.

At right is a steam shovel, and just ahead of it are several drill towers. Dynamite is placed in the drilled holes. After the charges are set off, the steam shovel will continue its progress forward, one shovel full at a time, clearing a path 40 feet wide and 12 feet deep.

The French built bridges across the Culebra Cut at Culebra, Empire, and Barbacoas. The tremendous effort by the French resulted in the removal of about 30 percent of the material at the Culebra Cut.

The Bucyrus steam shovel No. 228 at work at Culebra. Just ahead of it are drill towers preparing for dynamite charges. About 225,000 feet of pipe was laid in the cut to power the air drills. Air compressors were located at Río Grande, Empire, and Las Cascadas.

Everyone stops to look when a dynamite charge is set off. It was very hot working in the cut, sometimes referred to as Hell's Gorge. Daytime temperatures often exceeded 100 degrees and were sometimes as hot as 130 degrees.

West Indian sappers from Barbados and Jamaica performed most of the dynamite work. Some were killed in the process due to premature detonation, and so were some U.S. foremen. Many more people were killed in the recurring slides. About 60 million pounds of dynamite were used in the excavation of the Culebra Cut.

Steam shovels load four trains of about 20 dump cars each. This work went on from dawn to dusk. The collier trains would arrive in the evenings to fill the steam shovel bunkers with about 40 to 50 tons of coal each night. The repair trains were also active every night, maintaining the steam shovels and pneumatic drills.

This Bucyrus steam shovel, No.264, loads dump cars at Culebra. From 50 to 68 steam shovels operated in the cut every day. Though John Stevens originally ordered 100 Bucyrus steam shovels, by 1911, 88 Bucyrus shovels were at work on the canal, along with 23 Marion steam shovels, which arrived from Ohio that year. The 95-ton Bucyrus was best suited for the work at Culebra, and No. 123 set a record in March 1910 when it excavated 70,000 cubic yards in 26 days.

A special track crew of six men laid new track as the shovels progressed. About 275 miles of track was shifted every year without delaying the 160 spoil trains running every day. Besides moving track by hand, twelve specially developed steam cranes, called track shifters, were also used, moving entire track sections at a time.

The buckets of the 95-ton Bucyrus steam shovels held five cubic yards, about eight tons, or one large rock. They could load a dump car in just a few minutes. Steam shovel operators were some of the highest paid employees in Panama, receiving $210 per month. A shovel also required two firemen, a crane man or dump operator, and, of course, a train of waiting dump cars.

Bucyrus shovel No. 214 loads another rock. Between 150 and 160 trains of spoil pulled by full-size steam locomotives left the cut every day except Sunday. The total volume of material removed from the cut was 96 million cubic yards. On average, each shovel dug over a million cubic yards during the seven years of U.S. excavation.

Another train is loaded with spoil. There were 161 American steam locomotives pulling the dump cars, along with 146 French narrow-gauge locomotives. A total of 4,283 dump cars or flatcars with unloading plows hauled spoil from the cut. Note silver employee housing above the cut, at top right.

The Chagres River enters the Culebra Cut under the Panama Railroad bridge at Chagres Crossing, near Gamboa. A temporary dike diverted the Chagres during excavation of the cut. The Gamboa dike was finally dynamited on 10 October 1913, ending 30 years of shovel work. President Woodrow Wilson had the honor of detonating the dynamite charge via telegraph line from Washington, D.C.

Though the steam shovel work was finished, millions of cubic yards were excavated from the cut by dredges over the next few years. This was due to slide activity, the effects of which are shown here at Cucaracha in 1914.

A ladder dredge works at removing a slide at Cucaracha. In October 1914, two slides completely blocked the canal for nearly two weeks, and on 18 September 1915 a giant Cucaracha slide of 20 million cubic yards closed off the canal for seven months.

Slides at Cucaracha, nearby Gold Hill, Contractors Hill, and East and West Culebra have kept dredges busy since before the canal opened to the present day.

Another view of the slide at Culebra. Dredge crews worked to clear the slides, as ships waited at anchor to transit the canal. Shallow-draft ships were allowed to transit as soon as dredges had cleared enough of the debris.

On 15 August 1914 the Panama Railroad Company steamship *Ancon* became the first cargo vessel to officially transit the canal and locks from sea to sea. The *Ancon* was not the first vessel to transit the canal, as many transit tests were conducted before the canal was officially opened. The first vessel was actually a *cayuco* paddled by William Gorgas, Colonel Mason, and Joseph Le Prince of the sanitary department. Traveling in the summer of 1912 from the Pacific to the Atlantic, they had to portage around the unfinished locks.

The American-Hawaiian Steamship Company steamer *Missourian* transits the canal on 15 August 1914 with the help of a Panama Canal Company tug. On 18 and 19 May 1914, the canal handled its first commercial cargo. The American-Hawaiian steamer *Alaskan* arrived at Balboa with 12,000 tons of sugar and 2,000 cases of pineapples. Several bargeloads of sugar, in tow of the tug *La Boca*, made it as far as Pedro Miguel Locks. Then, in tow of another tug, the barges completed the trip to Cristóbal. The empty barges, in tow of the tug *Mariner* heading southbound, became the first continuous transit of vessels from sea to sea, arriving at Balboa on 19 May.

A four-masted bark in tow of two Panama Canal Company tugs heads through the Culebra Cut in 1915. By the time the Canal opened in 1914, commercial sail was nearly gone. Sailing ships made up only 1.5 percent of the total vessel transits during the first two years of the Canal's operation, and the last commercial sailing ship transited the Canal in 1932.

THE PACIFIC DIVISION

The Pacific division extended 11 miles and included the Pedro Miguel Locks, Miraflores Dam and Lake, Miraflores Locks, and the Pacific approach channel through the Río Grande valley and 4.5 miles into the Bay of Panama from La Boca. Sydney B. Williamson, head of the division, was at somewhat of a disadvantage in keeping up with other divisions, since work didn't begin until 1908. This was due to the change of plans enacted by Secretary of War William Howard Taft, for defense reasons. The original International Consulting Board plan of 1906 had planned a three-tier lock (as at Gatun) for the Pacific side between Sosa Hill and Corozal. A dam there would create a seven-square-mile lake. However, Taft strongly objected to this site so near the Pacific, arguing that it would be vulnerable to enemy shellfire. After about a year and a half of discussion, work finally began in December 1908 at the controversial new location, seven miles inland from the deep water of Panama Bay.

The Pacific division dredging fleet consisted of 34 vessels. The steam-powered, twin-screw ladder dredge *Corozal* (see pages 137-139) was designed to work in the mud, gravel, rock, and clay found in the Río Grande. The other seagoing dredge used here was the *Culebra*, the 2800 gross ton sister-ship to the *Ancon*, which was used in Limon Bay by the Atlantic division. Both were built by Maryland Steel Company. The *Culebra*, a suction dredge, worked in the seaward end of the approach channel. She was 288 feet long and 47 feet in beam, with a 25-foot depth of hold and a hopper capacity of 2,200 cubic yards. Her two 772-horsepower pumping engines powered two 20-inch dredging pumps capable of removing 15,000 cubic yards in a day. She toiled 24 hours a day, six days a week, and on Sundays her coal bunkers were filled at La Boca and maintenance work was performed.

Four 20-year old ladder dredges inherited from the French were rebuilt at Balboa in 1907. The dredges *Marmot*, *Badger*, and *Mole* excavated near La Boca. The suction dredge *Gopher* excavated 2,007,950 cubic yards of sand for concrete at Chame, in the Pacific about 25 miles southwest of Panama City. The lighter dipper dredge *Cardenas* worked alongside wharves and in areas the larger dredges found too restrictive. Nine self-propelled clapets, also inherited from the French, were rebuilt in Balboa and used on the Chame sand run and around La Boca. Six American-built tugs were used to tow barges and scows, and for shifting other equipment.

Drill barges were most important in dredging hard rock. The *Teredo*, 127 feet long and 32 feet in beam, with a 12-foot draft, had three 50-foot-tall drill towers. Each tower could lower an Ingersoll-Rand rock drill to a depth of 60 feet. After drilling holes in five-foot sections, the holes were filled with dynamite cartridges that were set off so the dredges could dig a little deeper. Another way to break up the seabed rock was to pulverize it with a ram drill. The *Vulcan* used a ram 56 feet long, weighing 22 tons, hammering the rock seabed to a depth of about two feet.

All this dredging was finished by August 1913, about the same time the most seaward lock was complete. On 31 August 1913 the temporary dike on the Pacific side was blasted away with 37,000 pounds of dynamite.

The spillway arches of Pedro Miguel Locks have concrete forms still in place. This view looking north shows Cerro Luisa (Luisa Hill) at upper left, with the village of Pedro Miguel at right.

The lock spillway arches form a picturesque view at Pedro Miguel (overleaf).

Looking north at the 60-foot-wide center wall of Pedro Miguel Locks, it appears as though work has stopped here for a short time. The operating tunnel will be installed inside the empty center space.

This was the new location of the Miraflores Locks, decided on after Secretary of War Taft objected to the original plan of a three-tier lock between Sosa Hill and Corozal. Looking towards Panama City and the Pacific, Ancon Hill can be seen at center right.

By 1912 the Miraflores Locks were a bustle of activity. Large chamber cranes, located in the lock chambers (in background at right), transported the concrete, rather than the cableways used at Gatun. These cranes weighed about 95 tons each. Mixed concrete was transferred to the chamber cranes by special railcars, which were shunted along tracks to the lock floors. The chamber cranes picked up the buckets and poured the concrete where needed.

The huge berm cranes, on gantries, were used in mixing concrete and were sometimes called mixing cranes. Weighing 470 tons, these berm cranes had towers measuring 40 by 50 feet, were 62 feet tall, and supported cantilevered arms that moved 2.5-yard buckets of sand and gravel to the hoppers, where they were mixed with cement and water to make concrete. Note the operator compartment, located under the crane arm.

Two berm cranes are shown at Miraflores. A chamber crane, at left, is working in the lock chamber. Both types of cranes were specially built by the Wellman-Seaver-Morgan Company of Cleveland, Ohio.

This view of the berm cranes shows, at right, piles of crushed rock from Ancon, with sand piled beside them. Dredged by the *Gopher* at Chame Point, sand was shipped by barge to Balboa, where it was transferred to railcars for delivery to the locks. Note the boxcars delivering cement to the concrete mixers, at the base of the berm cranes.

Workers prepare forms at Miraflores prior to receiving the buckets of concrete. A steam-powered electrical generator plant has just been constructed, upper right. Still in use today, it is now powered by diesel turbines. Just below the generator plant, piles of crushed rock and sand are stored on opposite sides of the rail trestle. Note railcars delivering sand and gravel, at left.

The chamber crane is ready to lift the concrete buckets from the flatcars at left, while berm cranes in the background continue to mix concrete. Water tunnel forms are being assembled at lower left.

Construction on the center wall at Miraflores continues. Note the narrow-gauge steam locomotive in the lock chamber. Steam-powered winches are located above the water tunnel forms, at left, to winch cable from the boom to aid in placement of forms and equipment. The chamber cranes in the background will move along the rails to this spot when it is time to pour concrete. A total of 2.5 million cubic yards of concrete was used in the construction of the Pedro Miguel and Miraflores locks.

Just south of Miraflores Locks is the Rio Grande delta area, Corozal, Diablo Heights, Balboa, and Panama Bay. This eight-mile approach channel was dredged by the ladder dredge *Corozal* and the seagoing suction dredge *Culebra*. The spoil was used to fill in the area at Amador, near La Boca. A breakwater continuing out to Naos, Culebra, Perico, and Flamenco Islands was constructed with spoil from the Culebra Cut. Fort Grant was located on the islands from 1913 through World War II and had more firepower than any other defense site. Fort Amador replaced it after the war. Ferries crossed here until the Bridge of the Americas was built in 1962.

Fort Sherman guarded the entrance on the Atlantic side. The fort is still in use today.(see pg. 174)

A rock quarry and a rock-crushing plant were located on Ancon Hill. Holes were drilled into the rock using pneumatic well drills and tripod drills (photo at left). The rock was then dynamited, and pieces were transported to the rock crusher by railcars using Lidgerwood unloaders. A No. 12 McCully gyratory crusher reduced the rock to chunks of five inches or less, and four No. 6 McCully crushers made smaller gravel. This was loaded by gravity into waiting railcars by way of 12 hand-operated chutes (above). This quarry site was later named Quarry Heights when the U.S. military took it over during World War I.

The steam-powered dipper dredge *Cascadas* of 1915, moored next to the Dredging Division administration building at Gamboa, was built by the Bucyrus Company of Milwaukee, Wisconsin, along with two sister-ships, the *Paraiso* and the *Gamboa* of 1913. The Cascadas is 144 feet in length with 56 feet of beam and a 16.6 foot hull depth. With a 15-cubic-yard bucket they could dredge to a depth of about 50 feet. Working at the canal from about 1915 until the 1990s, the *Cascadas* was to be scuttled because her working life was over. However, as the last surviving steam dredge from the construction era, she deserves to be preserved, and there are plans to restore her as a canal-dredging interpretive center.

The ladder dredge *Corozal* (above), 1,925 tons, was built by William Simons of Renfrew, Scotland, in 1911. This oceangoing dredge, with an overall length of 268 feet, a 45-foot beam, and a 19-foot depth of hull, was a side-casting bucket excavator. The spoils were sometimes cast into barges alongside, or straight overboard by way of the side shoot at right. She could also take 1,200 tons into the hopper via a center shoot, at the center of the photo. The *Corozal* had two triple-expansion steam engines of about 1,000 horsepower each, with Scotch marine boilers, used for both propulsion and dredging. Note the 25-ton bull wheel at center top, which drove the chain of buckets.

The 39 buckets used on the *Corozal* (next two pages) were of two sizes: 54 cubic feet for use in sand and silt, and 34 cubic feet for use in rock and clay. The lip or rim riveted to the top of each cast steel bucket was tempered manganese. The buckets revolved around a 100-ton, 115-foot-long adjustable ladder. In three years the *Corozal* removed 4,193,000 cubic yards of spoil from the Pacific channel.(See pg. 159)

THE AMERICAN ERA

On 18 November 18 1903 a treaty between the United States and the newly formed Republic of Panama was signed. It allowed the United States to construct, operate, maintain, and defend a canal across the Panamanian isthmus. In return, the U.S. paid Panama $10 million and agreed to an annual payment of $250,000. For $40 million, the U.S. purchased the rights and properties from the French, who had labored at constructing a canal from 1879 to 1899. The U.S. also purchased private property within the ten-mile-wide Canal Zone.

The canal ultimately cost the U.S. $352 million. The outbreak of World War I in early August 1914 pushed news of the opening of the Panama Canal off the front page. Due to the war and the frequent slides in Culebra Cut, the formal opening did not occur until 12 July 1920.

Over the years, Panama and the U.S. signed other treaties, including one in 1936 that increased the annuity to $430,000. The annuity eventually rose to $10 million plus 37 cents per ton of each transiting vessel. This totaled $104.6 million in 1996. On 10 August 1977 and 7 September 1977, two more treaties were agreed upon by Panama and the United States. The Carter-Torrijos treaties stated that the U.S. would give the canal and Canal Zone to Panama by 31 December 1999. The Neutrality Treaty of 1977 guaranteed that the canal will remain permanently neutral. In 1994 Panama amended its national constitution to ensure the operation of the canal would not be influenced by partisan political affairs.

The United States is justifiably proud of its construction of the "eighth wonder of the world," but also realizes it is time for Panama to control the canal, which has divided the country in two for nearly a hundred years. Though the U.S. has now completely left the Canal Zone, the treaties authorize U.S. government agencies to continue to provide support for Panama if deemed necessary.

Most Panamanians hope no outside help will ever be needed, and they are embarking on an ambitious program of upgrading the locks and canal. Many people have taken the attitude that "if it ain't broke, don't fix it," but Panama doesn't want to be left behind in the 21st century and is planning for the steady increase of shipping using the canal. Current projects include widening the Gaillard (Culebra) Cut from 500 feet to 630 feet; replacing the electro-mechanical gate-moving bull wheels and connecting rods with electro-hydraulic arms controlled by computer systems; rebuilding the 53,000 feet of towing track; increasing the number of Mitsubishi towing locomotives to 108; increasing the number of ship-assist canal tugboats to 24; replacing the 116 rising-stem valves and the 120 cylindrical valves, all mechanically operated, with hydraulically operated systems; converting to a computer-based control system; and building a new-generation traffic management system.

The original 40,43-ton electric towing locomotives or mules (top, at right) were designed by Edward Schildhauer and built by General Electric at Schenectady, New York, at a cost of $13,000 each. They were among the last pieces of equipment installed before the canal opened, running on five-foot track along the top of the lock walls. The locomotives are propelled by a 75-horsepower electric tractor motor at each end, with an electric motor powering the center-mounted towing cable windlass, which was capable of towing 25,000 pounds.

The 55-ton Mitsubishi locomotives (in the centre of the photo, bottom right, taken at Gatun Locks) replaced the GE mules about 1965 and have a 70,000-pound towing capacity using two windlasses. They have a single control cab and are propelled by a 170-horsepower electric motor that produces a higher top speed. The new-generation 55-ton Mitsubishi locomotives are propelled by a 290-horsepower electric motor and tow at an even higher speed of five miles per hour. Soon there will be a total of 108 locomotives in use.

The Gatun Dam spillway, at right, is located just southwest of the Gatun Locks and controls the level of Lake Gatun. The power generating house (center), capable of generating 6,000 kilowatts in 1914, supplied the electrical needs of Gatun Locks and nearby towns and shipyards.

On the top of the spillway are steel regulating gates of the Stoney type. These gates are designed to maintain the level of the lake between 80 and 87 feet above sea level, depending on season. They are shown here during the dry season. At left is the power house.

Miraflores Lake, between Pedro Miguel and Miraflores Locks, is fed by the Río Grande and Río Cocolí. To insure the lake level remains at 55 feet above sea level, a spillway was built at Miraflores Locks (above). The steel regulating gates are similar to the ones at the Lake Gatun spillway.

The range marker at Gamboa (left) marks the correct route for Gamboa Reach. Most of these original navigational markers are no longer used, replaced by newer range markers. At left is the Panama Railroad bridge. Note the wooden automobile deck added to the left side of the railroad bridge.

The control house at the Pedro Miguel Locks (top), like other control houses, is located on the center wall of the uppermost lock.

Transiting vessels wait their turn on Miraflores Lake (bottom) before proceeding through the locks. The ship at left is the *Cleveland*, a C5 break-bulk steamship of 600 feet in length. At right is a general cargo ship of approximately 500 feet. These vessels are dwarfed by the largest ships to transit the canal such as the 950-foot *Tokyo Bay* and the 972.7-foot ore carrier *San Juan Prospector*.

The lock gates at Miraflores Locks open after the ship has been lowered to sea level, to allow smooth progress to the Pacific Ocean.

The next two pages show the control board and the electrical panels, respectively. The control board for the two locks at Miraflores is smaller than the board for the three locks at Gatun, which measures 65 feet long. The upright indicators show the position of the rising stem valves, and the taller indicators show the water level in each lock. Interlocking bars underneath the controls prevent the operator from opening valves out of sequence. The aluminum handles must be turned in the proper order or they cannot be turned. If a valve is being repaired or should not be turned for some reason, it is very clearly tagged, as shown at the bottom of the photo.

The electrical panels are below the control boards and are laid out in an open manner for easy maintenance. The footstool allows access to the overhead wiring. Though the control board is the original design, the wiring and electrical motors have been updated. When originally constructed by the young GE company, these controls were considered the latest technology, and they still operate well today. However, there are plans to computerize the control system.

The Panama Canal Administration Building at Balboa Heights is located at the foot of Ancon Hill. The principal offices of the different divisions of the Panama Canal are still located here. The offices of the Panama Railroad were also located here when it was running.

The Balboa School is located just below the administration building. This school was for all grades, with the high school located on the third floor. In 1941 a high school was built across the street, and this school became known as the Balboa Elementary School.

The Panama Railroad shut down in the 1980s, so this station at Pedro Miguel is no longer used. In 1849 the number of men crossing the Isthmus on their way to the California gold fields made obvious the need for a trans-isthmian railroad. During that year (after a grant to a French syndicate had expired in 1848), William Henry Aspinwall, John L. Stephens, and Henry Chauncy, with their associates, incorporated the Panama Railroad Company. The government of New Granada (after 1861, Colombia) gave this company the exclusive right to build a railway. In 1867 a 99-year lease was granted for a quarter-million-dollar annual fee. Work on this incredibly difficult undertaking began in 1849 and continued for six years, with many lives lost. On 27 January 1855 a locomotive crossed the American continent for the first time.

Rolling stock sits abandoned near Gamboa today. Years ago the railway was vital to Panama and was considered the busiest line in the world. In 1910 the line moved 300 million tons of freight, in addition to 1.5 million passengers and Isthmian Canal Commission supplies. It also moved about 375,000 tons of rock and dirt spoil *every day*.

The Panama Railroad Company also operated three cargo steamers between Colón concession from the French and soon was responsible for moving the railroad above the level of the new Lake Gatun. This required re-laying 40 miles of the 47-mile line, at a cost of $8,866,392. There are plans for the passenger cars seen here to be restored some day.

Heavy-duty cranes are critical when maintaining locks, since individual gates weigh up to 745 tons. The venerable floating steam crane *Hercules* (at left), built in 1912, with hull dimensions of 150 by 88 feet, has a lifting capacity of 250 tons and worked with the crane *Ajax* prior to the arrival of the *Titan* (at right).

The steam crane *Titan* was built with three others between 1938 and 1942 by Deutsch Maschine Fabrik. A war prize obtained from Germany after World War II, she arrived on the east coast of America in 1946. With hull dimensions of 205 by 108 feet, the *Titan* just fits inside the locks, with 12 inches to spare at either side. With a lifting capacity of 350 metric tons, she was one of the most powerful cranes of her day. These cranes are based at Gamboa, for use anywhere along the canal.

This is another venerable steam crane that has been in use at the Panama Canal Company shipyard since it was built by American Hoist and Derrick Company in 1916. Originally steam powered, this crane travels on railway tracks and has been converted to diesel power.

The PCC shipyard was built during the construction era, and its graving dock has the same dimensions as the Panama Canal locks, 1,000 by 110 feet. It is now operated by Braswell Shipyard.

This 75-ton steam railway crane, No. 176, was built by the Bucyrus Company of South Milwaukee, Wisconsin. Designated No. 64 by the PCC, this model was not used to dig the Culebra Cut. It is one of the last surviving Bucyrus steam cranes in Panama.

THE
BUCYRUS Co
BUILDERS
SOUTH MILWAUKEE WIS.
No 176

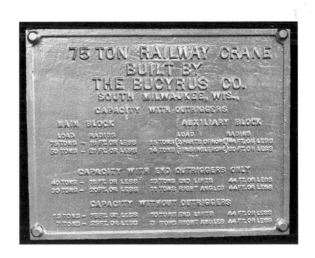

75 TON RAILWAY CRANE
BUILT BY
THE BUCYRUS CO.
SOUTH MILWAUKEE, WIS.
CAPACITY WITH OUTRIGGERS

MAIN BLOCK   AUXILIARY BLOCK
LOAD   RADIUS   LOAD   RADIUS
75 TONS - 19 FT. OR LESS   15 TONS (2 PARTS OF ROPE) 14 FT. OR LESS
50 TONS - 21 FT. OR LESS   14 TONS (1 TON WIRE ROPE) 30 FT. OR LESS

CAPACITY WITH END OUTRIGGERS ONLY
40 TONS - 18 FT. OR LESS   13 TONS END LIFTS   44 FT. OR LESS
30 TONS - 20 FT. OR LESS   11 TONS RIGHT ANGLES 44 FT. OR LESS
CAPACITY WITHOUT OUTRIGGERS
13 TONS - 19 FT. OR LESS   10 TONS END LIFTS   44 FT. OR LESS
7 TONS - 29 FT. OR LESS   3 TONS RIGHT ANGLES   44 FT. OR LESS

APPENDIX

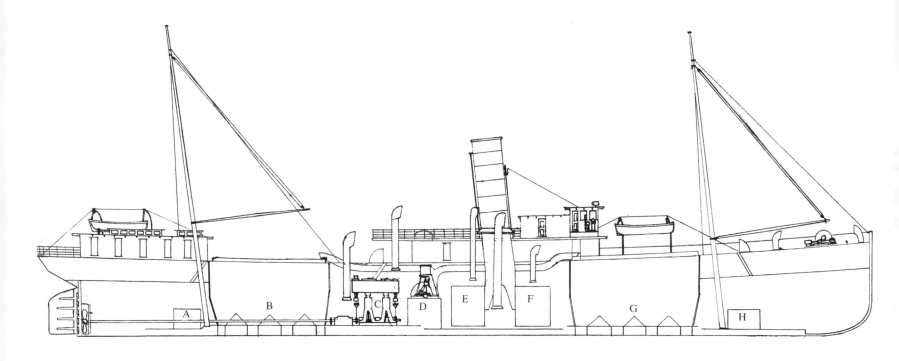

Sea-going suction dredge *Ancon*
inboard profile

A-Two 2,000 gallon tanks   E-2 boilers

B-Aft hopper   F-2 boilers

C-1,300 horsepower steam engine   G-Forward hopper

D-772 horsepower, 20 inch suction pump   H-Two 2,000 gallon tanks

The *Ancon* (later renamed *Caribbean*)and sistership *Culebra* were built in 1907 by Maryland Steel Co. of Sparrow Point, Maryland. They measured 2,800 gross tons, 288 feet in length, 47.5 feet in breadth, 25 feet in depth, with a 19.5 foot draft and a hooper capacity of 2,200 cubic yards. Their machinery consisted of two propelling engines of 1,306 horsepower, two engines of 772 horsepower powering two 20 inch dredging pumps, two drag engines, and four gate winding engines. Steam pressure was supplied by four boilers, capable of producing 3,390 horsepower.

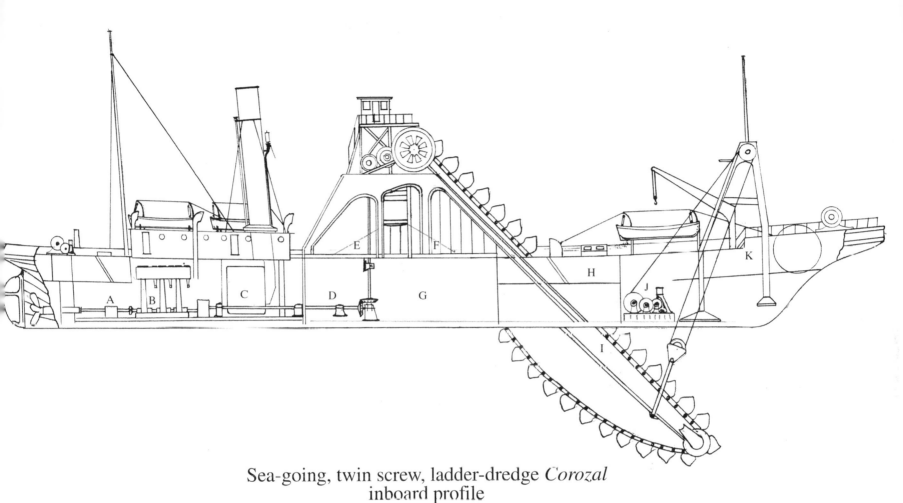

Sea-going, twin screw, ladder-dredge *Corozal*
inboard profile

A-Chainlocker
B-Steam engines
C-Boilers
D-Boiler feed tank
E-Main shoot
F-Slide shoot

G-Hoppers
H-Officers' and crews' quarters
I-115 foot long ladder and buckets
J-Ladder hoisting gear
K-Store

The Corozal was built by William Simons and Co. Ltd., of Renfrew, Scotland in 1911. She steamed from the Clyde River, Scotland through the Straits of Magellan to Balboa, over 12,000 miles, in 117 days. This was a record breaking voyage for a ladder dredge.

Measuring 268 feet overall, 1,925 gross tons, she had two triple expansion steam engines of 17, 27, and 43 inch cylinder diameters, and 27 inch stroke. Developing 928 and 965 horsepower with steam pressure of 180 lbs. p.s.i., they propelled the ship or powered the dredging equipment. The two Scotch marine boilers were 14.5 feet in diameter and 10.5 feet long with 2,022 square feet of heating surface. The cast iron propellers were 9.4 feet in diameter with 12 feet of pitch.

VESSELS OWNED BY THE PANAMA CANAL AND EMPLOYED BY THE PANAMA CANAL AND PANAMA RAILROAD CO.
FOR THE YEAR ENDED JUNE 30
1914

Name of vessel.	Class.	Material.	Gross tons.	Dimensions.			Built.		Purchased.		Estimated value.	Complement.		Where employed.
				Length.	Breadth.	Depth.	When.	Where.	When.	Where.		Officers.	Crew.	
PANAMA RAILROAD CO.				*Ft. in.*	*Ft. in.*	*Ft. in.*								
Advance*.....	Steam screw.	Iron...	2,605	295 0	38 4	23 4	1883	Chester, Pa.........			$250,000.00			Atlantic side.
Allianca*.....	...do.........	...do...	3,905	336 0	42 0	23 9	1886	.....do.........			400,000.00			Do.
Ancon[1]*.....	...do.........	Steel.	9,606	489 5	58 0	28 9	1902	Sparrow Point, Md.	1909		850,000.00			Do.
Colon[2]*.....	...do.........	...do...	5,667	360 0	50 0	32 2	1899	Philadelphia, Pa.	1905		650,000.00			Do.
Cristobal[3]*.....	...do.........	...do...	9,606	489 5	58 0	28 9	1902	Sparrow Point, Md.	1909		850,000.00			Do.
Panama[4]*.....	...do.........	...do...	5,667	360 0	50 0	32 2	1898	Philadelphia, Pa.	1905		650,000.00			Do.
No. 1.........	Lighter......	...do...	200	110 4	24 6	9 0	1896	Chester, Pa.........			5,000.00			Balboa.
No. 2.........	...do.........	...do...	275	111 8	24 4	9 0					5,000.00			Loaned to division canal transportation.
No. 4.........	...do.........	...do...	200	110 0	24 0	9 0					5,000.00			Balboa.
No. 7.........	...do.........	...do...	200	110 6	24 3	9 0					5,000.00			Do.
No. 8.........	...do.........	...do...	300	109 3	24 0	9 0					6,000.00			Do.
No. 9.........	...do.........	...do...	300	111 2	24 4	9 0					6,000.00			Do.
No. 10.........	...do.........	...do...	300	110 4	24 7	9 0	1905				8,000.00			Do.
No. 11.........	...do.........	...do...	300	110 4	24 7	9 0	1905				8,000.00			Do.
A.........	Coal lighter .	Iron...	200	115 0	24 6	7 11					6,000.00			Do.
B.........	...do.........	...do...	200	115 0	24 6	7 11					6,000.00			Do.
C.........	...do.........	...do...	200	115 0	24 6	7 11					6,000.00			Do.
D.........	...do.........	...do...	200	111 3	24 6	7 2					4,000.00			Do.
(No name)....	Pile driver...	Steel.		71 0	30 0	6 2	1909	Cristobal, Canal Zone.			8,000.00			Limon Bay.
Manzanillo....	Coal lighter ..	...do...	250	80 0	30 0	10 0	1910	.....do...			17,650.00			Manzanillo Bay.
Naos.........	Gas launch...	Wood.	11.15	40 0	10 0	5 0			1914		4,500.00			Balboa.
PANAMA CANAL.														
Division of canal transportation.														
Porto Bello[5]..	Tug.........	Steel..	227	126 0	23 5	14 5	1906	Baltimore, Md...	1907	Baltimore, Md.	55,000.00	4	26	Atlantic entrance.
Dixie.........	Gas launch...	Wood.	8	35 0	7 6	4 6	1910	Philadelphia, Pa.	1910	New York, N.Y.	4,000.00		2	Do.
Balboa.........	Tug.........	Iron...	67	60 0	12 0	8 0	1885	France.........		French Co......	10,000.00	2	3	Gatun Lake.
Mariner.........	...do.........	Steel.	234	113 0	25 6	13 6	1906	Camden, N. J...	1908	Galveston, Tex.	65,000.00	4	14	Atlantic entrance.
Periwinkle....	Gas launch...	Wood.	2.6	25 5	6 2	2 9		Morris Heights, N. Y.	1913	On Isthmus....	750.00		1	Pacific entrance.
Fortifications.														
No. 8.........	Deck barge...	Steel..	30	40 0	15 0	5 0	1906	Jacksonville, Fla.	1906	Jacksonville, Fla.	2,420.00			Atlantic entrance.
Aranal.........	Gas launch...	Wood.	6.25	32 2	7 4	4 1	1909	Philadelphia, Pa.	1909		1,400.00			Do.
Flamenco.........	...do.........	...do...	6.30	30 0	7 0	3 0	1912	New York, N. Y.	1912	New York, N.Y	2,435.00			Pacific entrance.
No. 61.........	Deck lighter..	Steel.	300	110 0	24 6	7 10	1906	Norfolk, Va......	1907	Panama R. R.	20,628.00			Do.
Vedette.........	Gas launch...	Wood.	6.76	32 0	8 5	4 1			1914					Atlantic entrance.
Division of erection.														
Flying Fish...	Gas launch...	Wood.	4.76	26 9	8 2	3 6			1914	Panama R. R..				Canal.
No. 6.........	Hopper barge.	Steel.	1,200	156 0	35 0	12 0	1908	Newport News, Va.	1908	Newport News, Va.	28,000.00			Do.

[1] Formerly st. s. Shawmut (117125).
[2] Formerly st. s. Mexico (92936).
[3] Formerly st. s. Tremont (145934).
[4] Formerly st. s. Havana (96435).
[5] Formerly st. s. Robert H. Smith (203112).
* Ocean-going vessels having an aggregate crew of 488 men and 100 officers.

Vessels Owned by the Panama Canal and Employed by the Panama Canal and Panama Railroad Company—Continued.

Name of vessel.	Class.	Material.	Gross tons.	Dimensions. Length.		Breadth.		Depth.		Built. When.	Built. Where.	Purchased. When.	Purchased. Where.	Estimated value.	Complement. Officers.	Crew.	Where employed.
Division terminal construction.				*Ft.*	*in.*	*Ft.*	*in.*	*Ft.*	*in.*								
No. 118	Dump scow	Wood	650	150	0	30	0	10	6	1911	Cristobal, Canal Zone.		Cristobal, Canal Zone.	$12,985.00			Atlantic entrance.
No. 2	Hopper barge	Steel	1,200	156	0	35	0	12	0	1908	Newport News, Va.	1908	Newport News, Va.	28,000.00			Do.
No. 3	do	do	1,200	156	0	35	0	12	0	1908	do	1908	do	23,500.00			Do.
No. 4	do	do	1,200	156	0	35	0	12	0	1908	do	1908	do	23,500.00			Do.
No. 5	do	do	1,200	156	0	35	0	12	0	1908	do	1908	do	28,000.00			Do.
No. 9	do	do	1,200	156	0	35	0	12	0	1908	do	1908	do	28,000.00			Do.
No. 11	do	do	1,200	156	0	35	0	12	0	1908	do	1908	do	28,000.00			Do.
No. 13	do	do	1,200	156	0	35	0	12	0	1908	do	1908	do	28,000.00			Do.
No. 14	do	do	1,200	156	0	35	0	12	0	1908	do	1908	do	23,500.00			Do.
No. 15	do	do	1,159	168	0	35	0	12	0	1908	do	1910	do	52,175.00			Do.
No. 16	do	do	1,159	168	0	35	0	12	0	1908	do	1910	do	52,175.00			Do.
No. 17	do	do	1,159	168	0	35	0	12	0	1908	do	1910	do	52,175.00			Do.
No. 18	do	do	1,159	168	0	35	0	12	0	1908	do	1910	do	52,175.00			Do.
No. 1	Derrick barge	Wood	360	96	0	42	0	8	6	1910	Cristobal, Canal Zone.			40,000.00			Do.
No. 2	do	do	360	96	0	42	0	8	6	1910	do			40,000.00			Do.
No. 8	Oil barge	Steel	30	40	0	15	0	5	0		Jacksonville, Fla.			2,420.00			Do.
No. 9	do	do	30	40	0	15	0	5	0		do			2,420.00			Do.
No. 12	Crane barge													25,000.00			Do.
Mary S	Steam launch	Wood	18	33	0	8	9	6	0	1908	Portsmouth, N.H	1908	Navy Yard, N.Y.	4,000.00			Do.
Bonita	Gas launch	do	6.15	32	0	7	0			1910	Port Clinton, Ohio			2,000.00			Do.
Coco Solo												1914					Do.
Mechanical division.																	
Ruth	Steam launch	Wood	20	36	0	8	10	6	1	1905	Portsmouth, N.H	1905	New York, N.Y	2,433.00	1	4	Atlantic entrance.
Q[1]	Launch	do	3	36	0	9	0	5	0	1903	New York, N.Y.	1903	do	3,000.00	2		Pacific entrance.
Health department.																	
Santa Rita	Gas launch	Wood	7.92	35	3	7	3	4	2					4,500.00			Pacific entrance.
Pratique	do	do	2	32	0	7	0	2	0	1908	Baltimore, Md	1908	Baltimore, Md.	1,300.00			Do.
Psyche	do	do	7.92	35	3	7	8	4	8	1912	Philadelphia, Pa.	1912	New York, N.Y	4,000.00	1	2	Atlantic entrance.
Division of civil affairs.																	
Chagres	Gas launch	Wood	4.6	23	9	6	8	2	3	1911	Cristobal, Canal Zone.			638.00			Gatun Lake.
Lirio	do	do	8.77	32	3	7	3	3	9	1911	New York, N.Y.	1911	New York, N.Y	2,328.00			Cristobal.
Barbacoas	do	do	4.46	28	4	7	0	3	0			1907	Panama R. R.	270.00			Balboa.
Division of meteorology.																	
Snail	Gas launch	Wood	4.26	26	2	6	6	2	8								Gatun Lake.
Auditing department.																	
San Lorenzo	Gas launch	Wood	1.48	18	9	5	3	2	6	1911	Cristobal, Canal Zone.			227.00			Culebra Cut.
Dredging division.																	
No. 3	Deck barge	Steel	115	75	0	25	0	7	0	1906	Jacksonville, Fla.	1907	Jacksonville, Fla.	8,800.00			Atlantic side.
No. 5	do	do	115	75	0	25	0	7	0	1906	do	1907	do	8,800.00			Culebra Cut.
No. 6	do	do	115	75	0	25	0	7	0	1906	do	1907	do	8,800.00			Atlantic side.
No. 7	do	do	115	75	0	25	0	7	0	1906	do	1907	do	8,800.00			Do.
No. 101	Mud scow	do	400	126	0	31	0	10	6	1908	Newport News, Va.	1908	Newport News, Va.	26,083.00			Culebra Cut.
No. 102	do	do	400	126	0	31	0	10	6	1908	do	1908	do	26,083.00			Do.
No. 103	do	do	400	126	0	31	0	10	6	1908	do	1908	do	26,083.00			Do.
No. 104	do	do	400	126	0	31	0	10	6	1908	do	1908	do	26,083.00			Do.
No. 113	do	do	400	126	0	31	0	10	6	1908	do	1908	do	26,083.00			Do.
No. 114	do	do	400	126	0	31	0	10	6	1908	do	1908	do	26,083.00			Do.

[1] Formerly launch Panama.

Name of vessel.	Class.	Material.	Gross tons.	Dimensions.			Built.		Purchased.		Estimated value.	Complement.		Where employed
				Length.	Breadth.	Depth.	When.	Where.	When.	Where.		Officers.	Crew.	
Dredging division—Con.				*Ft. in.*	*Ft. in.*	*Ft. in.*								
No. 115	Mud scow	Steel	400	126 0	31 0	10 6	1908	Newport News, Va.	1908	Newport News, Va.	$26,083.00			Culebra Cut.
No. 116	....do	...do	400	126 0	31 0	10 6	1908	.....do	1908	....do	26,083.00			Do.
No. 117	....do	...do	400	126 0	31 0	10 6	1908	.....do	1908	....do	26,083.00			Do.
La Valley	Crane boat	Iron	1,200	160 0	40 0	15 0	1887	Scotland		From French Co.	23,500.00	2	14	Do.
No. 2	Clapet	...do	690	136 6	26 3	14 6		.....do		....do	20,000.00	2	14	Do.
No. 4	....do	...do	710	140 3	26 6	14 6		.....do		....do	20,000.00	2	14	Atlantic side.
No. 12	....do	...do	660	138 6	25 6	15 10	1887	Jarrow, England		....do	20,000.00			Culebra Cut.
No. 1	Ladder dredge	...do	580	112 0	29 6	11 6	1887	Belgium		....do	35,000.00			Chagres River.
No. 3	Clamshell dredge.	...do	580	112 0	29 6	11 6	1908	Cristobal, Canal Zone.						Culebra Cut.
No. 4	18-inch pipeline dredge.	...do	580	112 0	29 6	11 6	1910	....do			153,261.00	11	58	Atlantic side.
No. 5	Ladder dredge	...do	580	112 0	29 6	11 6	1887	Belgium		From French Co.	35,000.09	5	40	Culebra Cut.
House boat										....do				Atlantic side.
Do										....do				Paraiso.
Mindi	Dipper dredge	Steel	520	110 0	38 0	11 0	1906	Chicago, Ill	1906	Featherstone Foundry & Machinery Co.	100,000.00	4	27	Culebra Cut.
Chagres	....do	...do	510	110 0	38 0	11 0	1907	Cristobal, Canal Zone.	1907	Atlantic, Gulf & Pacific Co.	102,500.00	4	27	Do.
No. 82	20-inch pipeline dredge.	...do	670	124 3	36 6	9 0	1908	Sparrow Point, Md.	1908	Maryland Steel Co.	98,550.00	11	58	Do.
No. 83	....do	...do	670	124 3	36 6	9 0	1908	.....do	1908	....do	98,550.00	11	58	Do.
Sandpiper	....do	...do	670	124 3	36 6	9 0	1908	.....do	1908	....do	98,550.00	11	58	Atlantic side.
No. 86	....do	...do	940	150 0	40 0	10 6	1910	Baltimore, Md	1910	Baltimore, Md	160,000.00	11	58	Culebra Cut.
Caribbean [1]	Seagoing suction dredge.	...do	2,800	288 0	47 6	25 0	1907	Sparrow Point, Md.	1907	Maryland Steel Co.	362,425.00	9	57	Atlantic side.
Azimuth	Gas launch	Wood		23 2	6 6	2 6					500.00			Culebra Cut.
San Blas	....do	...do	5	32 0	6 0	4 0	1908	Baltimore, Md	1908	Baltimore, Md	1,300.00		1	Do.
Toro Point	....do	...do	4	28 0	5 6	4 0	1910	Cristobal, Canal Zone.			1,469.00		1	Atlantic side.
Luis	....do	...do		15 0	4 6	1 6		....do			355.00		1	Chagres River.
San Lorenzo	....do	...do		18 9	5 3	2 6	1911	....do			227.00			Gatun Lake.
Margaret	....do	...do		32 0	7 0		1910	Port Clinton, Ohio			2,000.00			Culebra Cut.
No. 60	Deck lighter	Steel	300	110 0	24 6	7 10	1906	Norfolk, Va	1907	Panama R. R. Co.	10,000.00			Do.
No. 62	....do	...do	300	110 0	24 6	7 10	1906	.....do	1907	....do	10,000.00			Atlantic side.
No. 63	....do	...do	300	110 0	24 6	7 10	1906	.....do	1907	....do	10,000.00			Culebra Cut.
No. 64	....do	...do	300	110 0	24 6	7 10	1906	.....do	1907	....do	10,000.00			Atlantic side.
No. 65	....do	...do	300	110 0	24 6	7 10	1906	.....do	1907	....do	10,000.00			Culebra Cut.
Pile Driver No. 1.	Pile driver	Wood	95	60 0	30 0	4 0	1906	Cristobal, Canal Zone.	1906	Merrill, Stevens & Co.	2,500.00			Do.
Gatun [2]	Tug	Steel	164	101 0	22 0	22 6	1902	Philadelphia, Pa.	1906	New York, N.Y	42,000.00	4	26	Do.
Bohio [3]	....do	...do	171	104 0	21 0	21 6	1905	Camden, N. J.	1908	Norfolk, Va	57,000.00	4	26	Do.
De Lesseps	....do	Iron	98	67 6	15 0	9 0		Cristobal, Canal Zone.		From French Co.				Chagres River.
Empire	....do	Steel	288	120 0	24 0	14 6	1909	Port Richmond, N. Y.	1909	Port Richmond, N. Y.	75,500.00	4	26	Culebra Cut.
No. 20 [4]	Dump barge	...do	1,200	156 0	35 0	12 0	1908	Newport News, Va.	1908	Newport News, Va.	28,000.00			Do.
No. 21 [5]	....do	...do	1,200	156 0	35 0	12 0	1908	.....do	1908	....do	28,000.00			Do.
No. 4	....do	...do	400	122 0	31 6	10 6	1908	Balboa, Canal Zone.	1908		24,300.00			Pacific side.
No. 5	....do	...do	400	122 0	31 6	10 6	1908	.....do	1908		24,300.00			Culebra Cut.
No. 6	....do	...do	400	122 0	31 6	10 6	1908	.....do	1908		24,300.00			Do.
No. 7	Sand barge	...do	500	127 6	32 0	12 0	1909	.....do			20,000.00			Pacific side.
No. 8	....do	...do	500	127 6	32 0	12 0	1909	.....do			20,000.00			Culebra Cut.
No. 9	....do	...do	500	127 6	32 0	12 0	1909	.....do			20,000.00			Chagres River.
No. 10	....do	...do	500	127 6	32 0	12 0	1909	.....do			20,000.00			Do.
No. 11	....do	...do	500	127 6	32 0	12 0	1909	.....do			20,000.00			Pacific side.
No. 12	....do	...do	500	127 6	32 0	12 0	1909	.....do			20,000.00			Culebra Cut.
No. 13	Dump barge	...do	500	154 0	32 0	10 7	1910	.....do						Do.
No. 14	....do	...do	500	154 0	32 0	10 7	1910	.....do						Do.
No. 15	....do	...do	500	154 0	32 0	10 7	1910	.....do						Do.
No. 16	....do	...do	500	154 0	32 0	10 7	1910	.....do						Do.
No. 17	Coal barge	...do	250	110 0	24 0	7 6					2,666.00			Atlantic side.
No. 18	....do	...do	250	110 0	24 0	7 6					2,666.00			Culebra Cut.

[1] Formerly Ancon.
[2] Formerly st. s. H. B. Chamberlain (96649).
[3] Formerly st. s. Jack Twohy (201823).
[4] Formerly barge No. 1 (Atlantic division).
[5] Formerly barge No. 7 (Atlantic division).

Name of vessel.	Class.	Material.	Gross tons.	Dimensions. Length.	Breadth.	Depth.	Built. When.	Where.	Purchased. When.	Where.	Estimated value.	Complement. Officers.	Crew.	Where employed
Dredging division—Con.				*Ft. in.*	*Ft. in.*	*Ft. in.*								
No. 19	Wrecking barge.	Steel		112 2	29 6	11 6								Culebra Cut.
Machine shop	Barge	do	75	110 0	24 0	7 6								Pacific side.
Bruiser	Pile driver	do		60 6	29 4	4 1								Do.
No. 1	Oil barge	do	50	81 6	18 6	7 6								Do.
No. 1	Clapet	do	408	133 6	25 1	11 0		England		England	$2,666.00			Atlantic side.
No. 6	do	do	450	133 6	25 1	11 0		Scotland		do	22,500.00			Pacific side.
No. 7	do	do	450	133 6	25 1	11 0		do		do	22,500.00			Do.
No. 8	do	do	450	133 6	25 1	11 0		do		do	22,500.00			Do.
No. 9	do	do	450	133 6	25 1	11 0		do		do	22,500.00			Do.
No. 10	do	do	450	133 6	25 1	11 0		do		do	22,500.00			Do.
No. 11	do	do	408	133 6	25 1	11 0		do		do	22,500.00			Culebra Cut.
Mole	Ladder dredge	do	500	170 0	26 0	12 0		do		Scotland	54,000.00			Do.
Gopher	do	do	500	170 0	26 0	12 0		do		do	54,000.00			Pacific side.
Badger	do	do	400	112 2	29 6	11 6		Belgium		Belgium	65,000.00			Do.
Marmot	do	do	400	112 2	29 6	11 6		do		do	65,000.00			Culebra Cut.
Cardenas	Dipper dredge	do	300	110 0	38 0	11 0	1906	Balboa, Canal Zone.	1906	New York, N.Y	94,500.00			Do.
Culebra	Seagoing suction dredge.	do	2,800	288 0	47 6	25 0	1907	Sparrow Point, Md.	1907	Baltimore, Md.	330,000.00			Pacific side.
Corozal	Ladder dredge	do	260	260 0	45 0	19 6	1912	Scotland	1912	Canal Zone	299,340.00			Culebra Cut.
Coal hoist	Bucket dredge	do	100	72 4	18 0	7 2								Atlantic side.
Birdena	Steam launch	do	25	60 0	12 0	8 0	1885	France	1904	From French Co	4,500.00			Culebra Cut.
Louise	do	do	25	60 0	12 0	8 0	1885	do	1904	do	4,500.00			Pacific side.
No. 26	do	do	20	55 0	12 0	7 0	1885	do	1904	do	4,500.00			Culebra Cut.
Pathfinder	do	Wood	4.5	28 0	5 0	3 6	1907	United States	1907	United States	400.00			Pacific side.
Skidoo	do	do	4.5	28 0	5 0	3 6	1907	do	1907	do	400.00			Culebra Cut.
Vulcan	Rock breaker	Steel	200	100 0	28 0	8 0	1908	Scotland	1908	Scotland	50,000.00			Pacific side.
Teredo	Drill barge	do		112 0	36 0	8 0	1909	Balboa, Canal Zone.						Do.
La Boca [1]	Tug	do	192	120 0	24 0	13 0	1907	Camden, N. J	1907	New York, N.Y	57,600.00			Culebra Cut.
Cocoli [2]	do	Steel	213	96 0	23 0	12 4	1904	Philadelphia, Pa.	1907	do	57,600.00			Do.
Chame [3]	Tender	do	180	105 0	20 3	14 0	1899	Hull, England	1907	Canal Zone	25,000.00			Do.
No. 1	Gas launch	do	0.5	15 0	4 0	2 6	1907		1907	do				Pacific side.
No. 2	do	do	0.5	15 0	4 0	2 6	1907		1907	do				Culebra Cut.
No. 3	do	do	0.5	15 0	4 0	2 6	1907		1907	do				Do.
No. 4	do	do	0.75	28 0	5 0	3 6	1907	Balboa, Canal Zone.	1907	do	300.00			Do.
No. 5	do	do	0.75	28 0	5 0	3 6	1907	Hull, England	1907	do	300.00			Do.
Miraflores	Tug	do	206	118 6	23 0	12 6	1910	Wilmington, Del.	1910	Wilmington, Del.	65,000.00			Do.
Reliance [4]	do	do	272	134 0	25 0	13 6	1906	Camden, N. J	1908	Newport News, Va.	44,605.00			Do.
Bolivar	do	do	234	127 1	23 2	9 5	1885	Philadelphia, Pa.			28,000.00			Pacific side.
Sanidad [5]	Tender	do	221	82 10	15 6	11 6	1884	Tyne, England	1904	From French Co	23,095.00	2	5	Culebra Cut.
No. 2	Coal-hoist barge.	do		75 0	25 0	6 0								Do.
Unnumbered	Diving barge.	Wood		18 0	6 0	2 0								Do.
Do	do	do		18 0	6 0	2 0								Pacific side.
No. 136	Barge	Steel	2,000	160 0	50 6	13 6	1913	United States	1913	United States	61,000.00			Culebra Cut.
No. 137	do	do	2,000	160 0	50 6	13 6	1913	do	1913	do	61,000.00			Do.
No. 138	do	do	2,000	160 0	50 6	13 6	1913	do	1913	do	61,000.00			Do.
No. 139	do	do	2,000	160 0	50 6	13 6	1913	do	1913	do	61,000.00			Do.
No. 140	do	do	2,000	160 0	50 6	13 6	1913	do	1913	do	61,000.00			Do.
No. 141	do	do	2,000	160 0	50 6	13 6	1913	do	1913	do	61,000.00			Do.
Unnumbered	Oil barge	do		82 10	14 10	6 2								Atlantic side.
Do	do	do		72 4	18 0	7 2½								Pacific side.
No. 22	Sand barge	do	1,200	156 0	35 0	12 0	1908	United States	1908	United States	13,627.55			Do.
Unnumbered (2).	Barges	do		30 0	14 6	4 0								Culebra Cut.
Unnumbered	Barge	do		30 0	14 6	4 0								Pacific side.
No. 3	Water barge	do	50	81 6	18 6	7 6								Do.
Unnumbered	do	do		82 10	14 10	7 2½								Atlantic side.
Do	do	do		82 10	14 10	7 2½								Culebra Cut.
Gamboa	Dredge	do		144 0	44 0	16 6	1913	United States	1913	United States	257,186.00			Do.
Paraiso	do	do		144 0	44 0	16 6	1913	do	1913	do	257,186.00			Do.
Search	Launch	Wood	16.3	45 0	9 0	4 7	1913	do	1913	do	7,010.59			Do.
Pioneer	do	do	13.19	40 0	8 0	4 0	1913	do	1913	do	6,452.25			Do.
Patrol	do	do	13.19	40 0	8 0	4 0	1913	do	1913	do	6,552.25			Do.
No. 85	Dredge	Steel	670	124 3	36 1	9 0	1908	do	1908	do	42,987.50			Do.
No. 6	Launch	Wood	4.5	28 0	5 0	3 6	1907	do	1907	do	400.00			Do.
Unnumbered (7).	Scows, pontoon.	do												Do.

[1] Formerly st. s. E. G. Reynolds.   [2] Formerly st. s. Catherine Moran.   [3] Formerly British st. s. Riversdale.   [4] Formerly st. s. M. E. Scully.   [5] Formerly water boat No. 2

PHOTOGRAPH NOTES

The photographs in this book were made by Gerald Fitzgerald Sherman in April 1912, and Jeremy Sherman Snapp in January 2000, with these exceptions: Trevor Townsend Snapp made the photo of Tobago, page 167, middle, and the photo of the operating tunnel, page 172, middle. January 2000. Seven photos on pages 113 through 119, of the Culebra Cut, were made by J.W.W. in 1914, and were acquired by my grandfather, John Farrington Snapp, during a Panama Canal transit in 1918. John Snapp made the photograph of the USS *Oregon* in 1918, on page 8 and the two photographs of Gerald Sherman on page 11.

The photographs on the following pages were made by Gerald Fitzgerald Sherman, April 1912: 25, 27, 28, 29, 31, 32, 33, 34, 35, 36, 37, 38, 39, 41, 42, 48, 49, 50, 51, 54, 55, 57, 58, 59, 60, 61, 62, 63, 64, 65, 66, 67, 68, 69, 70, 71, 72, 73, 74, 75, 76, 77, 78, 79, 80, 81, 82, 83, 84, 85, 86, 87, 88, 89, 90, 91, 92, 93, 94, 95, 96, 97, 99, 100, 101, 102, 103, 104, 105, 106, 107, 108, 109, 110, 111, 112, 121, 122, 124, 125, 126, 127, 128, 129, 130, 131, 132, 133, 134, 135, 136, 137, 138, 139, and 167T.

The photographs on the following pages were made by Jeremy Sherman Snapp, January 2000: 5, 10, 17, 18, 19, 20, 21, 22, 23, 24, 25, 26, 43, 44, 45, 46, 47, 52, 53, 141T, 141B, 142, 143, 144, 145, 146T, 146B, 147, 148, 149, 150, 151, 152, 153, 154, 155, 156, 157T, 157BL, 157BR, 167T, 167B, 168T, 168B, 169T, 169B, 170T, 170B, 171T, 171B, 172T, 172B, 173T, 173M, 173B, 174T, 174M, and 174B.

BIBLIOGRAPHY

BOOKS

Abbot, Willis J. Panama and the Canal in Picture and Prose. New York, NY: Syndicate Publishing Co., 1913.

Alexander, Fran, et al. (editors). *Oxford Encyclopedia of World History.* New York, NY: Oxford University Press, 1998.

Anderson, Willard V., editor. *Ships and the Sea.* Milwaukee, WI: Kalmbach Publishing (quarterly), 1950s.

Barry, Tom and John Lindsay-Poland. *Inside Panama.* Albuquerque, NM: Resource Center Press, 1995.

Cameron, Ian. *The Impossible Dream.* New York, NY: William Morrow & Co., 1972.

Canal Zone. *August 15, 1914: The Panama Canal–Its 25th Anniversary. August 15, 1939.* Mount Hope, Canal Zone: Panama Canal Press, 1939.

Chidsey, Donald Barr. *The Panama Canal: An Informal History.* New York, NY: Crown Publishers, 1970.

Doggett, Scott. *Panama.* Hawthorn, Australia: Lonely Planet Publications, 1999.

Friar, William. *Portrait Of The Panama Canal.* Portland, OR: Graphic Arts Center Publishing, 1999.

Keller, Ulrich. *The Building of the Panama Canal in Historic Photographs.* New York, NY: Dover Publications, Inc., 1983.

Lee, W.Storrs. *The Strength to Move a Mountain.* New York, NY: Putnam, 1958.

Mack, Gerstle. *The Land Divided: The History of the Panama Canal and Other Isthmian Projects.* New York, NY: Alfred Knopf, 1944.

Mahan, Alfred Thayer. *The Influence of Sea Power Upon History 1660-1783.* Boston, MA: Little, Brown and Co., 1890.

Marshall, Logan. *The Story of the Panama Canal.* L.T. Meyers, 1913.

McCullough, David. *The Path Between The Seas: The Creation of the Panama Canal 1870-1914.* New York, NY: Simon and Schuster, 1977.

Meditz, Sandra W. and Dennis M. Hanratty (editors), Federal Research Division. *Panama: A Country Study.* Washington DC: Superintendent of Documents, U.S. Government Printing Office. 1989

Padelford, Norman Judson. *The Panama Canal In Peace and War.* New York, NY: Macmillian Company, 1942.

Panama Canal Commission. *The Panama Canal: A Vision For The Future.* Panama Canal Commission, 1997.

Sauer, Carl Orwif. *The Early Spanish Main.* Berkeley, CA: University of California Press, 1966.

Shaw, James L. *Ships of the Panama Canal.* Annapolis, MD: United States Naval Institute Press, 1985.

Siegfried, Andre. *Suez and Panama.* New York, NY: Harcourt and Brace and Co., 1940.

Smith, Darrell Hevenor. *The Panama Canal: Its History, Activities, and Organizations.* Baltimore, MD: John Hopkins Press, 1927.

United States Department of Commerce. Bureau of Marine Inspection and Navigation.*Merchant Vessels of the United States.* Washington, DC: United States Government Printing Office (annual), various years.

Weir, Hugh C. *The Conquest of the Isthmus.* New York, NY: G.P. Putnam's Sons, 1909.

Note: Much of the information in the sources above came from the following contemporary periodicals:

Bulletin du Canal Interoceanique. French. Nos. 1-127, 1879-1889.

Canal Record. American. Vols. I-IX, 1908-1916.

PERIODICALS

Chester, Colby M. (Rear Admiral, USN). "The Panama Canal." *National Geographic Magazine.* Vol. XVI, No. 10. Washington, DC: National Geographic Society, October 1905.

Edwards, Thomas Edwin. "Peacock and Panama." *Sea Breezes.* No. 1 Vol. 1. Isle of Man, UK., December 1919.

Marden, Luis. "Panama, Bridge of the World." *National Geographic Magazine.* Vol. LII, No. 11. Washington, DC: National Geographic Society, November 1941.

Shaw, James L. "Sailing Ships and the Panama Canal." *The Sea Chest.* Seattle, WA: Puget Sound Maritime Historical Society, September 1986.

Shonts, Theodore P. (Chairman ICC). "The Panama Canal." *National Geographic Magazine.* Vol. XVII, No. 2. Washington, DC: National Geographic Society, February 1906.

Showalter, William Joseph. "The Panama Canal." *National Geographic Magazine.* Vol. XXIII, No. 2. Washington, DC: National Geographic Society, February 1912.

MAPS and CHARTS

Collins, K. St. B. (Rear Admiral, OBE, DSC), Superintendent. *Admiralty Chart No. 1299* London, UK. Published at the Admiralty, 1957, with corrections to 1988 and 1999.

Inter American Geodetic Survey, U.S. Army and Hydrographic Office. Sheet (map) Nos. 4244 III, 4243 IV, 4243 III, 4243 II, 4242 I. Washington, DC: Defense Mapping Agency, Hydrographic-Topographic Center 1976-77, in collaboration with Instituto Geographico Nacional "Tommy Guardia," Panama City, Panama. Updated 1987, 1997, 1998.

Index

Ladder dredges.

Island of Tobago, near Panama City.

French cemetery at Gatun.

General Electric plate on all 1914 mules.

Bell from French vessel.

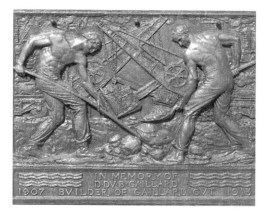

David Gaillard memorial plaque.

Goethals monument, Balboa Heights.

Bell from SS *Ancon* on stairs of Panama
Canal Administration Building

Tobago ferry *Islamorada*, of 1912.

French built steam launch
Hyacinth, of 1883.

Fishing boat at San Lorenzo.

Suspension bridge,
Río Nombre de Dios.

Woman in traditional *pollera* dress.

Lock gate 40-horsepower drive motor.

1,000-foot-long lock operating tunnel.

Lock gate bull wheel, 20 feet in diameter.

Panama Railroad tanker
car hauled fuel oil.

Industrial Brownhoist
steam railway crane.

Model of Lidgerwood dirt spreader
at Miraflores Locks.

Beachfront barracks at Fort
Sherman, on Limon Bay.

American Western flatcar of 1908,
had 18 cubic yard capacity.

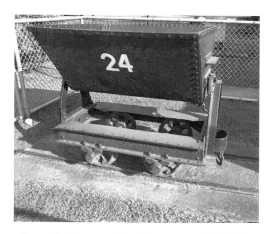

French Decauville dumpcar of 1889,
had capacity of .66 cubic yard.